THE RED DEVIL

THE RED DEVIL

To Hell with Cancer — and Back

KATHERINE RUSSELL RICH

CROWN PUBLISHERS

NEW YORK

Grateful acknowledgment is made to the following for permission to reprint
previously published materal:

Condé Nast Publications: Portions of "Fight" and "Rock" originally appeared in
Allure. Copyright © 1997 by Condé Nast Publications. All rights reserved.
Reprinted with permission.

Hal Leonard Music: Excerpt from "Cruisin'," words and music by William
"Smokey" Robinson and Marvin Tarplin. Copyright © 1979 by Bertam Music
Company. All rights controlled and administered by EMI April Music, Inc., on
behalf of Jobete Music Co., Inc. All rights reserved. International Copyright
Secured. Used by permission.

New Issues Press: "Variations on My Room in the Bone Marrow Unit" from *The
Woman With a Cubed Head* by Julie Moulds. Copyright © 1998 by Julie Moulds.
Reprinted by permission of New Issues Press.

D. Nurkse: "How We Are Made Light" by D. Nurkse. Reprinted by permission
of the author.

Published by Crown Publishers,
201 East 50th Street, New York, New York 10022.
Member of the Crown Publishing Group.
Random House, Inc. New York, Toronto, London, Sydney, Auckland
www.randomhouse.com

CROWN is a trademark and the Crown colophon is a registered
trademark of Random House, Inc.

DESIGN BY KAREN MINSTER

Printed in the United States of America

Library of Congress Cataloging-in-Publication Data
Rich, Katherine Russell.
The red devil : to hell with cancer— and back / by Katherine
Russell Rich. — 1st ed.
1. Rich, Katherine Russell—Health. 2. Breast—Cancer—Patients—
United States Biography. I. Title.
RC280.B8R53   1999
362.1'9699449'0092—dc21
[B]   99-25516
ISBN 0-609-60321-3

10 9 8 7 6 5 4 3 2 1
First Edition

To
Henry and Sally Creech

PART ONE

PART TWO

PART THREE

PART ONE

When we stand
on the low rungs
of the ladder of sorrow,
we cry.
When we come
to the middle
we're silent.
But when we climb
to the top
of the ladder
of sorrow,
we convert sadness into song.

—ancient Hebrew poem

CRITICAL MASS

I FOUND THE LUMP TWENTY MINUTES BEFORE BREAKFAST, three weeks after my marriage broke up. I was taking a shower, soaping myself down, when my fingers slid into it and stopped. They pushed on a little, flew off, returned to confirm that, yes, there was something hard and alien in my left breast. After a pause, they resumed their investigation. But now my brain had seized up, and so the information my fingers were attempting to relay remained stalled, unprocessed, in touch. Perhaps that's why I retain such a strong sense memory of what they found: a mass the size of a pigeon's egg, a blob that felt like oatmeal packed in casing. I was puzzled—the thing hadn't, I swear, been there the day before—but not perplexed. I knew instantly what it was.

At work I phoned a friend. "Michelle," I whispered. "On top of everything, I found a lump in my breast. I can't do it: I can't go on!" Those were the days when I still liked hyperbole, before an excess of real drama killed my taste for the manufactured kind.

My friend soothed and reassured me; she presented the facts: All women find lumps; I was only thirty-two; the odds were this was absolutely nothing. The case she constructed was sure and ordered. "Yeah, you're right," I agreed, allowing myself to be seduced into calm, willing, temporarily, to forget my certainty, illogical as it was.

My evidence, had I spoken it, was this: My life was spinning to hell; my marriage had busted up at the end of August; I'd promptly moved eleven cartons of possessions into a sublet where I wasn't supposed to smoke but I did; and now, in September, I was about to take a new job. Of course that lump was cancer. What else was it going to be?

And those were my surefire arguments. If I wasn't going to bring them up, I certainly wasn't going to mention that, six months before, in a journal, I'd written, "I can't stay in this marriage any longer. If I do, I'll get cancer." Or how, not long after, I'd experienced some weird psychic breast cancer flash. "Diego, I'm not kidding, I'm getting the strongest feeling that somebody in one of our families has it," I'd told my husband. "To be safe, why don't you call your mother down in Buenos Aires and tell her to get a mammogram." Spooked, she rushed to get the test, which came back normal.

Nor did I mention another recent occurrence, but only, I would have told you then, because it had slipped my mind. Fear, I realize now, was blocking the memory of how, a few months earlier, in bed, my husband had frozen while caressing me. "I don't want to scare you," he said softly, "but I think I found a lump here." When he tried to locate it again, it wasn't there. I chalked the incident up to projectile hypochondria.

Diego and I were absolute opposites about a lot things, and illness was one of them. "Ah! I think I have a cancer!" he would announce, lying prostrate on the bed. "What a baby," I'd say, not at all amused or compassionate. My father was a Christian Scientist, and while my mother insisted on raising my brother, sister, and me Episcopalian, his beliefs suffused the house. We weren't expected to deny disease as he was, but we were strongly encouraged to rise above it. "It's just mortal error," my father would counsel me when I was laid low by some ailment. I didn't have a clue what he was talking about, but I did know that mortal error was the reason why, in tenth grade, for instance, shimmery with a fever from bronchitis, I was still expected to haul myself to school. Coming into the adult world, I assumed everyone was like this. Diego, for one, was not.

"I have a headache! I cannot move," he declared from the floor of the Denver airport on Christmas Eve, where he'd flung himself just as the extended family was about to transfer to a flight to Breckenridge for a ski vacation. Pedestrians stepped over him. My parents stared down, flabbergasted. They'd never seen behavior like this. I had, a couple of times.

"Just ignore him," I advised my mother.

"But Kathy," she said. "He really looks sick."

"He is," I sneered. "Sick in his head."

I'd met Diego when he was thirty-one and I was twenty-five, at a party he threw at his apartment on East Fourteenth Street. When I'd rung the bell, he'd opened the door and done a double take. I was pleased by his show of interest, but I had to look away, for if he was thunderstruck, I was more so. He was blond and all-boy, sexy like a rugby player, and though I'd heard from our mutual friend that he was Argentine, I noticed he spoke with a slight twang, like someone out of Texas.

The inflection puzzled me for a long time, till I realized he'd picked up his American listening to Bob Dylan. As for his English, he'd learned that while attending a private Irish school in Buenos Aires, after which he'd gone on to study architecture for a few years before being sidetracked by marriage, two sons, and a job at a radical newspaper. Journalism in the States can be a high-risk profession, but in Argentina in the seventies, it was flat-out dangerous, particularly when practiced at a left-wing publication. The far-right government was waging a Dirty War against any-one who disagreed with its positions, and journalists as a group were high on the hit list. Students and intellectuals were being dragged from their homes in the middle of the night and brought to detention centers, where they were tortured and frequently killed. After a number of Diego's friends had been disappeared, his name turned up in some wrong address books and the police detained him twice. In the year before he fled the country, he got used to sleeping with a pistol under his pillow.

"This is where we kept the guns," he said four years later, while removing venetian blinds from their holder in order to help me hide my engagement diamond. Had I been better versed in self-help books, or common sense, I might have recognized that as a red flag: *Ask yourself—does he dislike his mother? Does he show signs of having blown up a building? Is he cold and distant to your pet?* But I was deeply impressed. Now, here was a man who'd had to fight for his beliefs, not like the wimpy American guys I knew. Not like, come to think of it, me.

As a child of the seventies, I'd grown up in thrall to the myth of the sixties, forced to make do with the insipid cultural signifiers of my own era. The seventies never rose any higher than glitter rock, Birkenstocks, and whippets as the drug of choice—unless you want to count those flashing disco ceiling balls. It was a bust decade all around, everyone agrees. And I'd been so close; just five years older, and I would have been right there, right in the thick of free love and social upheaval. I could have run away to Haight-Ashbury, slept on the floor of a crash pad, and gotten high with a rock band. Sure, the getting high part was still open to me, but otherwise, I had to settle for pathetic Woodstock rematches at places like the Pocono speedway. Big whoop, as we said in the Philadelphia area. I couldn't even go to Earth Day, man. I was grounded.

Having burned to taste the foment of the sixties, I romanticized Diego's experience of it, despite the ugliness of the South American version. When I looked at the photographs of the disappeared friends that he kept up on the wall, I saw credentials of cool, not the visible signs of trauma that they actually were. I ignored the fact that his nerves were jagged and his mood swings wide, that he spent hours in the dark watching Nazi war documentaries.

In that first languorous summer after we met, he courted me with games of Scrabble. I didn't even mind that he almost always won. He went to England and sent me postcards that made me laugh. He began bringing his sons over and I was struck by what a devoted father he was—even though once I stopped by and found the three of them sitting down to a meal of potato chips, pretzels, and peanuts; bachelor dinner. He was funny and smart, an artist and an outlaw, and I was desperately in love. I wanted to be an artistic outlaw, too. Too bad if he was a divorced, Catholic, leftist South American, which is how my traditional, Protestant-bred parents viewed him. I didn't care. I was marrying him.

As the big day approached, we couldn't quite see eye to eye on the matter of wedding attire. He wanted my dress to be red, to show my "solidarity with the Communist Party." I declined, pointing out that I was not, in fact, a Communist. Then he was adamant that I not put on a veil. "They symbolize the oppression of women," he said. Had I thought of the argument on my own, I would have been passionate about it. But I was in no mood, as the bride, the star, to have some half-baked Communist dictate wedding details. Even if he was my husband-to-be. "If a woman is forbidden to wear a veil by a man on the grounds of oppression, doesn't that sort of subvert the point?" I argued. In the end, I came down the aisle in basic bridal white and a small pillbox hat to which I'd attached some netting, in order to show that I had a mind of my own. It didn't cover my eyes, though.

No doubt the lump was there, in some form, on my wedding day, for according to studies, it would have needed seven years to grow to its final size. I can't say. I felt fine. But if it did exist, it was smaller than a half thought—it was a fleck, a scritch, a particulate mote. It would have been so puny, an immune system running on half-jets could probably have taken it out. There is a theory that all of us have cancer, that it develops in us all the time, but that, when working, our immune systems rear up and clobber it before it can grow. It's only when the immune system is suppressed, by stress, say, or some external agent, that the malignant cells are free to multiply into aggressive, hungry snarls.

There's another theory that some of us are born with a predisposition toward cancer, with marked meat for DNA. Many geneticists of this belief are careful to add that it's not a matter of nature versus nurture. The cancer gene doesn't have to be a predetermined death sentence, the current thinking goes. Even if one is carrying the gene, it may very well be possible to keep it deactivated by steering clear of damaging influences. In other words, scientists have finally begun to indict mind *and* body as culprits in cancer, to acknowledge that they work in concert. It's only taken them about 350 years to begin to mend the Cartesian split.

Genetic testing wasn't around at the time of my marriage, but if it had been, I would have been a prime candidate. "We have cancer all through the family," my mother told me after my diagnosis, and when I began to piece it together, I saw that we did: maternal grandmother, a tumor near the spine, which in the end killed her; paternal grandmother, breast cancer, which didn't, although it did require a mastectomy; great-grandmother, colon; uncle on mother's side, merkle cell sarcoma; skin cancers on both sides of the family; prostate on father's. In hindsight I see I should have done everything in my power to avoid carcinogenic factors. Instead I built my life around them.

I smoked, two packs of Newport Lights a day. (Smoking between ten and nineteen cigarettes per day increases a woman's chances of contracting breast cancer fivefold, according to a Swiss study published in 1998; as far as I know, nobody's tested for forty.) So did Diego, Camels. (Women who were exposed to someone else's smoke for just one hour a day over a year tripled their odds; same study.) I drank, a lot. ("At least fifty studies have indicated that alcohol may play a role in the development of breast cancer," a recent Reuters health service report observed. One found that women in their twenties who had fourteen or more drinks per week were at a 30 percent higher risk. Fourteen was during a week when I had the flu.) I ate like shit: *chiles relenos*, cheeseburgers, fish filets, occasional greens, frequent desserts. (Italian researchers who studied some twenty-five hundred women with breast cancer from 1991 to 1994 found a link between saturated fat, alcohol [again], and starch, and increased risk.) I worked out when I felt like it, which was hardly ever. ("Women who exercise at least four hours a week reduce their chances of getting breast cancer by at least 53 percent"; a 1997 Norwegian study, published in *The New England Journal of Medicine*.)

And mostly, I inhaled stress. ("Psychological stress diminishes natural killer cell and T-cell activity"; study conducted at Ohio State University, 1997, and while no one can say for sure what role a stressed immune system plays in cancer, I'd bank on it not being a good one.) It turns out, I wasn't destined to be one of those people who, upon reviewing the crack-up or bad patch in their life, says, "But from the outside, things looked fine." Nope, even from the outside, things looked kind of stretched. Each weekend, we had the boys, nine and five at the time of the wedding, which engendered the usual stepfamily strains. And yes, both our careers were blooming: He kept trading up, from reporter at UPI to head of Latin American operations at a television news service to executive news producer at a Spanish-language TV station; I switched from associate editor at an outdoors journal to senior editor at a travel magazine, a move that took me on trips to Hawaii, Tokyo, Rio, all over the place. But these were high-drive, adrenylated jobs that left us buzzed in the off hours, depleted of energy for each other.

Whether it was because of our temperaments or the configuration of our lives together, by the end of the first year, the marriage had pitched into continual rounds of battles and angry silences, intercut with occasional sweet, peaceful weeks that functioned as loss leaders back into the cycle. We fought about when his kids would come; we fought when his kids did come. We fought when, at a Chinese restaurant, he announced, "I cannot talk. I am in a trance," and refused to utter another word. ("He has the personality of a bad Rumanian film director," I scribbled furiously in my journal that night.) We fought about the trivial and the consequential: I complained about his singing tango music in the shower. He, in the heat of the moment, referred to my sister's baby, born with heart damage, as "that loser." We fought about his workaholism, my workaholism, about money, sex, vacations, anything.

"Hawaiian hamsteak," he insisted one night when a new couple was over and we were trying to decide where to eat. "I only go to places with Hawaiian hamsteak on the menu." It didn't take Stanley Morse for me to break the marital code: *I'm not spending the night in some overpriced Yuppie restaurant, which is, by the way, where these two look like they belong.*

"That's not true," I hissed. "Come on! You eat sushi." *Are you crazy? We are not going to any coffee shop. How often do we have people over? Can't you just act normal one time?*

No, he could not. At least not by my lights. Having married Diego because he wasn't like anyone I knew, I was seized by an urgent need to make him just like everyone I knew. I inexplicably wanted the kind of life I'd been trying to avoid before, a life with 401(K) plans, a co-op, all the codified, easily read measures of accomplishment. What had I been thinking, wanting to lead an artistic life, to link up with a man who could engage in a joint life of the mind?

I don't know when I began to lose my self, but at some point I did. Polarization set in, causing us, toward the end of the marriage, to harden into parodies of ourselves. The initial chemistry that attracted us became some awful, reverse alchemy that transformed us into stereotypes. By year five, the final year, I was a stiff-lipped, bloodless, manners-obsessed WASP. He was Ricky Ricardo in a bad mood. We were both miserable.

The curious thing, as I see it now, is not that this happened—it was pretty standard Jungian shadowboxing, the stuff of all bad marriages—but that I didn't leave. It would have been so easy—I had a decent job, savings. I had the emotional and financial wherewithal, and I was choking on unhappiness. Why didn't I just go?

But I stayed. I stayed because I still loved him and because I was locked in by obsession; I was consumed with setting things right. In our bedroom I'd lie on the bed and contemplate the mustard-gas-colored walls and catalog my grievances. Always, I'd arrive at the same conclusion: He had to change. He had to; it was the only way.

Night after night, the neurons raced that one pathway, carving it deeper in my brain. Obsession is the same thought repeated over and over till it blocks off reason, till it leeches sanity. And cancer is a single cell that reproduces uncontrollably till it grows so large, it starves the tissue around it and, ultimately, destroys its host. Both are repetitive, aberrant, both thrive in airless environments. One kills the body, the other, the spirit.

If there's a link between cancer and obsession—and, of course, the metaphysics of disease is tricky, unscientific as it is—I wouldn't have known to make it, not consciously, anyway. But in some dark, primal brain recess, the connection was becoming insistently clear. The last six months of the marriage, I was terrified all the time. Anxiety kept me braced and rigid; insomnia left me brittle. For reasons I would have ascribed to the circumstances, I felt like I was dying. It's terrifying now to look back and know that, actually, I was.

By the summer of 1988, at the age of thirty-two, I had embarked on the process of dying.

On some level, in some way, I knew it ("If I stay, I'll get cancer") and was desperate for help. The lump that had been there, a silent partner, for the whole of the marriage was now nudging itself into my consciousness, making itself known in glimmer signals that would flare up and fade away. I couldn't read them. I could only detect their vague afterimages. I could sense I was in danger, that something was wrong, ominous, but then again, my marriage was crashing down, and wasn't that how you were supposed to feel?

There was no last straw that caused the crash, only a catalyst: Pablo, his oldest, moved in with us. It was only going to be for a few months, but the living arrangements—two overgrown teenagers and one real one—were impossible. Soon the apartment itself seemed to be cracking from the tension. Spider lines and boils appeared in the ceiling, paint flaked down. The front lock fell apart. The VCR wouldn't tape. Every night I'd come home to find the answering machine blinking a wrong number. Some mixed-up lowlife was calling and leaving messages, oblivious to the recording. "I lent you the hundred bucks. I want the hundred bucks. I'm coming to get the hundred bucks," he'd threaten, his voice sounding like Danny DeVito's in *Throw Momma from the Train*.

Our fights grew wicked, thunderous.

"I think you should find another husband," Diego said quietly after one bruiser. "You're still young enough. You could."

I knew he meant it. I knew he was right. That night, he slept on the living-room floor, near Pablo on the futon. In the bedroom I cried so hard, breath wouldn't come. I stayed up almost till dawn, rocking to try and quell the sorrow, my body tight with grief, curving into the future that was inevitable. Then pulling back again.

I managed to hang on a few more months, then I couldn't anymore. I found an affordable sublet and packed my stuff. Just before I left, I slipped off my wedding band and hid it behind the bed, hoping Diego would happen on it in some later day and be pierced with sadness. In case he got over me too soon.

My brother and a friend came to help with the cartons. I thought I was forging ahead, moving into my new life. But, really, I was entering Cancerland.

BEAT

MY FIRST TIME OUT WITH CANCER, IT WAS LIKE BEING IN the middle of dismantling a rickety house and having a gas main explode underneath. I might have been prepared to dodge collapsing walls. I wasn't expecting to be plunged into a sinkhole.

The Salvadorans have a saying: The struggle is in the song. If so, my initial upsets were expressed through Terrence Trent D'Arby. *Wishing well, kiss and tell, ahhhwaaaahhwaahh . . .* After settling into the sublet, I played the tape maniacally, twenty, thirty times a night.

"I can't imagine what my neighbors think," I told my friend Sara.

"They're thinking, Get that girl laid," she said.

I was trying, I was trying, but without much success. The knowledge of the lump kept me chaste. What if someone, a near stranger, were to find it? What would I say? What would he?

"Excuse me. Are you aware that there's something as big as a walnut here?"

"Yeah, kind of."

"And have you called a doctor about it?"

"Yeah, kind of."

In fact, I had. In mid-September, I'd shut my office door and dialed my internist, a doctor by the name of Steve Altman. I whispered what the trouble was, asked what I should do.

"Are you getting your period?" he said.

I was, but—

"Oh, well, then. Everyone gets lumps right before their period," he said. "How old are you? Thirty-two? That's pretty young. It's probably nothing. Why don't you wait a month, and if it's still there, call me again. But if you're *really* concerned, you can come by. I'll feel your breasts anytime you want me to."

I'll feel your breasts anytime you want me to. I couldn't believe he'd said that. I'd just spent days living with the sharp, instinctive knowledge that I had cancer. It had taken days of steeling myself to make that call. I was terrified. He was hustling me off the phone with a joke. And he'd set it up so that if I insisted on an appointment, it was tantamount to requesting a feel. In my post-breakup state, I was already worried that, along with losing my husband, I'd lost respectability, some marital shield that prevented men from making snarky sexual comments. Well, check it out: Men were. I decided to drop the matter for a while. The guy was a doctor. He'd said not to worry. Fine. That's what I'd try to do.

Not always successfully. "I think this thing is cancer," I told the therapist I'd begun seeing around the time my marriage was breaking up.

"You don't have cancer," she said with surprising finality.

"I don't?" I said.

The therapist was in her seventies, one of the last of the unrepentant Freudians. "You'll find out what your issues are," the woman who recommended her had said. For a year, I'd been taking the couch and discovering that my issues appeared to be incredibly trivial. My mother hadn't bought me Barbie's clothes, she'd sewn them—the horror. The flu had prevented guests from attending my second-grade birthday party—the pain. When I suggested we speed it up, the Freudian chuckled. "People always think there are shortcuts," she said. "There aren't. Analysis takes time."

The lump, it became obvious, was not destined to be one of my issues. "You're too young," she said decisively when I brought it up again, her voice sounding a little strangled back there behind my head. Her reaction might have been reflexive. Among her patients, I'm sure she counted many who worried inordinately about odd lumps or blotches. Hours of listening to illness obsessives ("I know they're telling me it's nothing, but then why can't anyone explain why I see a faint penumbra when I stand?") must have led her to devise some all-purpose explanations.

Or her abrupt response might have been personal. The woman was in her cancer years. From the shaky tone in her voice, I got the impression the subject scared her silly. Or maybe she didn't know how to respond. Freudian analysis becomes flaccid, even laughable, when presented with the stiff, immediate requirements of a cancer diagnosis, of, for instance, chemo. Freudians, it could be said, are ill-equipped to deal with anything invented after Freud.

October rolled around. That pigeon's egg was still there. Briefly, I thought of phoning Altman back. But having waited a month as directed, I was—big coincidence—premenstrual once more. Wouldn't he just tell me I was getting my period again? I decided not to call. The urgency that was goading me earlier had eased, for urgency that's not acted on loses its insistence, re-forming itself into anxiety.

Nearly two months had passed since I'd first found the lump, enough time for it to have grown 20 percent larger. (The average breast tumor, studies show, doubles every 260 days.) It didn't occur to me that, if what I had was cancer, then what I had was a mass of rapidly dividing cells. I didn't know squat about medicine, didn't understand I was taking a risk by waiting. But the thought might have crossed my internist's mind. "You know," an oncology nurse told me years later, "the disease may have spread because he wouldn't see you. Did you ever think of that?"

I hadn't, not till she said it.

And now I try, as much as I can, not to.

By October I was well practiced in trying to persuade myself I was leading the good life. As a child, I'd known how to do this instinctively. Now it required forethought and brashness. It didn't come naturally. The good life was a stretch.

I got myself sent on assignment to St. Bart's, where I was put up at a tony hotel and where, one evening after dinner, I jumped in the pool in a black polyethylene miniskirt, at the urging of another member of the press crew. At a disco before dawn, I corralled a gorgeous French man in a white linen suit and made him drive me to the airport for the sunrise. Look at how wild and glamorous my life has become, I told myself, watching the lazy revolutions of the ceiling fan in my cottage—if Diego could see me.

Back in New York, I regarded the glittering view from my sublet, an aerie on the twenty-third floor. Diego is staring at an airshaft, I would think, while I'm gazing down on all of Manhattan. Ha! All right, so the apartment came with a hitch or two. I had to clear out whenever the lessor returned to town, which worked out to an annoying one week per month spent camped on a friend's floor. And the lessor was a bit on the neurotic side. I'd had to sign a two-page contract when I moved in, agreeing, among other things, not to knock down any dividing walls and to erase all signs of my existence for the weeks when she'd be in residence, put all my things in suitcases and stow them in the hall closet. Even my towels had to go. But the place also came fully furnished, which gave me the illusion that, by taking temporary possession of someone else's books and television and linens, I'd taken temporary possession of someone else's life. The stage-set quality of the arrangement pleased me. It was instructive. Newly engaged, the apartment's owner was just vacating the single life I was moving into. I paid careful attention to the artifacts she'd left behind. The framed photographs of her trips to China and Japan gave me heart. Her books, with titles like *Are All the Good Ones Taken?*, gave me pause.

As did the fact that the apartment was in the building where the actual *Waiting for Mr. Goodbar* murder had taken place. It didn't seem like a good omen.

I ignored the arrangement's drawbacks. They were only annoying and, besides, I had fresh concerns. I'd just had a fifth interview for a position I wanted, a job as a senior editor at a men's magazine. The editor had made it clear he was going to hire me, yet he continued to ask me back for still one more long, boozy lunch at the Four Seasons. We were going on four months. Even his company was confused. "Do you know what's taking him so long?" the personnel woman called to ask. I didn't, but I did know one thing: If I was sick, I wanted to get out of the job I was in. My editor there had limited sympathy for people in crisis. "I don't care about her dead husband," she'd actually snapped once when an employee, one month into widowhood, screwed up a project. If death itself didn't faze her, I didn't want to know how she'd handle a mere deadly disease. True, I had been getting warnings that the other place was kind of a boys' club, but I figured I could handle that. I wasn't exactly a girly girl. All in all, better to take my chances with the new boss, I decided, than to get stuck where I was with a preexisting condition.

I quit smoking, started running, but not for health reasons. "There's a man I'd like to fix you up with," the apartment's owner said on the phone from Los Angeles. "But he's a cardiologist. He won't go out with you if you smoke," she added, in what was no doubt a ploy to ensure I wouldn't burn holes in her wraparound sofa. I bit. The date never materialized, but I managed to give up cigarettes. It was the first signal I'd sent my body in years that I wanted to live.

Soon I'd embarked on a Bataan dating march. "There's this guy . . ." someone would say. "Great," I'd answer. *Bring 'em on.*

I went out with an ophthalmologist, a rock critic, a claims adjuster for the electric company. We went to lectures, to inns in the country, to Italian restaurants. At first I liked each person because he wasn't Diego. By the end of the evening, I'd hate him on the same grounds. I should have taken time off, learned to be alone, but shock had blasted me back onto a teenage emotional trajectory. The more men, the more it was clear you were attractive.

I resumed operating under principles that had been deep-frozen in my head around eleventh grade, that had been set down by my Virginia belle of a mother. Foremost was that if you didn't have a boyfriend, you were floating, undefined, unsettled and unsettling. If I'd been honest with myself, I'd have admitted I hated dating—even the name was preposterous—but that wasn't the point. I was resolutely living the good life, and the good life, if you were single, included dates. Besides, when I was out, I wasn't alone in the sublet, where the silence could grow so dense and cold, it chilled the walls.

Around this time, someone I met at a book party said that when she got divorced, she'd spent hours staring at herself in the mirror. I tried. It didn't help. Loneliness burned me. My marriage had been consuming in its intensity. Coming out of it, I needed a fleet of friends and I only had a few.

I managed a brief romance, with an alcoholic shrink. His drinking appealed to me. It made him less observant. He would come up and we would open a bottle of Scotch and by the time we'd decide to skip dinner, his words would be slurred. I liked that he wouldn't have noticed if my head had fallen off. It meant I didn't have to worry he'd find the lump. It also meant he was unreliable. An hour into an evening once, his face assumed a stricken expression. "I have to go home and clean my apartment," he said without further explanation, and walked out. "The man left the scene of a date," I said the next day, attempting to sound witty, the way someone leading the good life I was would talk. *What an asshole*, is what I thought.

A bad relationship was perfect for getting my mind off the breakup. My old obsessive tendencies kicked in, the contained ache helping to obscure the deeper, riveting pain it panicked me to feel. To shut it out, I lost myself in Michelle Shocked, in Toni Childs. *Rain come down, rain come down, come down on me.* I'd switched musical allegiances. Terrence Trent D'Arby was too giddy, I realized. He wasn't good at mournful regret.

The shrink's visits were becoming less frequent, but when he came by, I matched him glass for glass in Scotch. The next morning, shaky, I'd eat a candy bar to jack myself back up. Some days it worked. Some days I was so fine-tuned, I could rev myself with breath. Some days were heady. I'm swimming in light, I thought, trying to put words to the sensation. It really feels like I'm swimming in light. But not all of them were lucent. On the hard dark ones, breath could fracture me. Misery weighted my step but was useless in filling emptiness. Those days, I withdrew into air. I escaped into the hollow in my body.

And *hollow* was the operative word. Had I not been such a corporeal stoic, I might have been more alarmed by the exhaustion that had begun to slam me down, by the odd way my body was dissolving, like magic. In a few months, I'd lost thirteen pounds—a tenth of my weight. I chalked it up to a mix of insane hours and grief. The physical loss is expressing my emotional loss, I explained to myself; a new, more compacted me is being sculpted into existence.

But I never thought these things at the same time I thought about the lump, because the lump scared the holy bullshit out of me.

In November a curious thing happened. On the night before my thirty-third birthday, I was lying in bed, face to the wall, crying. Despondence had burned off the Scotch I'd drunk, was propelling me into hysteria. Between sobs, I'd go rigid, and it was in one of these moments of silence that I sensed a presence in the room behind me. Startled, I turned my head and saw a diffuse violet light shining through the bedroom door. The light didn't scare me, it soothed me, in fact, and within seconds, I was calm. Puzzled by this sudden well-being—the tears weren't even dry— I tried to work myself back into hysteria, but couldn't. My anguish had vanished, drained by the light. A sense of security overtook me, the first I'd felt in years, and soon I was asleep.

I hadn't yet read the philosopher William James's *The Varieties of Religious Experience*, which was written at the turn of the century and is full of stories like this. "Quite early in the night I was awakened," a correspondent of James's reports. "I felt as if I had been aroused intentionally, and at first thought some one was breaking into the house. . . . I then turned on my side to go to sleep again, and immediately felt a consciousness of a presence in the room, and singular to state, it was not the consciousness of a live person, but of a spiritual presence. This may provoke a smile, but I can only tell you the facts as they occurred to me."

If I had been familiar with the book, it might have been a comfort, for the facts as they occurred to me left me unhinged. I still can't account for them. I'm willing to concede that a combination of stress and Scotch may have produced the vision, that perhaps inner turmoil caused an optimistic aspect of my personality to split off into hallucination. I'd been under the influence of pressure and drink before, however, and the only result was a hangover. But if forced to explain, what I would say is that heading into a hellish midnight, on the eve of my thirty-third birthday, I was suddenly thrust into transcendence on a rush of absolute grace. Ten years on, the memory remains indelible, still potent and still inexplicable.

At the end of November, the job offer came through. I extracted a month off between jobs and booked a seat on a pre-Christmas flight to Breckenridge, Colorado, where my sister had moved to mourn the death of a child and to live for a time as a ski bum. On the way out, I calculated my fortunes: first the Caribbean, then the Rockies, next a great new job—boy, was my life turning around. In more ways than I would have wanted to admit. As the week wore on, I tried to overlook the fact that, though my sister had scared up some free lift tickets for me, I had no energy to use them. Mornings, I'd take a desultory pass at the bunny slope, try one, maybe two halting runs, then by lunch be back in bed. Peeling off ski clothes, I'd get under the covers and allow the mattress to suck me down. By the time my sister returned from her ski-shop job, around four, I'd be up and dressed again. I hadn't said anything about the lump. It wouldn't have been right. She was still twisted up over Katie, who'd died the January before, two weeks after turning one. With the anniversary upon her, my sister was shivery with grief. She lit candles in remembrance and left them burning all night. I worried about a fire. I worried about her. "I was walking through the woods this morning, and out of nowhere, I saw a young girl," she told me. "I know it was Katie, coming back."

I was cautious in our conversations. There were too many wrong things that could be said. On automatic edit, it was easy to omit mention of the naps.

"Let's go out," my sister would say in the evening. "Someplace nice for dinner."

"I'm kind of tired," I'd beg off. "Plus, it's so cold out here."

I hated to leave the condo after dark. With no fat left to pad me, the freezing night air cut like steel. So we'd stay home and I'd make my excuses by nine. Or I'd drag myself out and have a miserable time, too cold and too tired to stay completely awake.

Early in January the new job began. On the first day, I arrived to flowers on my desk, and a card that said, "That was the longest foreplay in magazine history. Glad you finally came." Oh man, I thought, recalling that, before coming into respectability, the editor had put out a skin magazine. *Oh man*. I poked the arrangement away, till only the tops of some freesia showed behind a pile of books.

A few hours later, the editor stopped by. "Did you get my flowers?" He grinned, holding the door frame and leaning in.

"Yes. I did," I said, my tone flatter than a dead rose.

He waited. I didn't smile. Silence froze us into place. He stared at me. I examined his shoes—one was crossed over the other, both had been recently shined—and finally he said, "Well . . ." The word thawed us and he walked away. When for the rest of the week, he avoided me, I saw it had been a tactical error to behave so coolly.

Two weeks into the job, insurance still pending, my company sent me for a free physical, at a place called the Life Renewal Institute. The work-up was thorough: an EKG, blood tests, eye and ear check, breast exam. During the palpation, the gynecologist instantly found the lump, which was no great surprise. By now you could actually see it, a visible swelling that was jutting against the skin. As her fingers circled in, I looked away, bracing for pandemonium. I thought for sure she'd halt the exam, race to the phone, and place a worried call to a colleague. "Could Dr. Breastexpert please stop by?" But all that happened was she asked if I knew it was there, suggested my own doctor take a look, and as I retied my gown, directed me to the next specialist. At the conclusion of my rounds, I was handed a report informing me I had a "1.5 cm lump in the upper left quadrant" of my left breast. As revelation, this news wasn't staggering. Nor was the follow-up advice: "The patient should see a doctor on an ongoing basis for continued monitoring." Flipping to the last page, I saw the lump hadn't even affected my final score. "General health: Good," the report concluded. Okay, I thought—maybe I was worried about nothing. I had it in writing: A whole squad of doctors had just pronounced me fine.

January ground on. My dating life faltered. Friends were running out of candidates, although I couldn't have said that I minded. The novelty of my new single life was wearing off and my luck hadn't been great. The men had ranged from the ridiculous to the porcine, although I'm sure I wasn't always much better. "I don't have fun," I said indignantly to one poor guy who'd simply asked what I liked to do for entertainment. Neither did he that night.

I'm not doing this anymore, I swore after another bad evening. A woman I didn't know well had arranged for me to have dinner with a Texas oilman, French by birth. "Great," I'd told him on the phone. "I'm working on a story about Paris, so maybe I can ask you some questions."

At the restaurant, I discovered he was as handsome as promised—"a lean Arnold Schwarzenegger," the go-between had said. But he was also notably self-regarding, even in respect to food. "The portions here are huge. Let's split a plate," he said as we took up the menus. The place served nouvelle Chinese. The portions were meager. When ours came, he laid into it fast, before I could get a fork in edgewise. I wasn't having better luck with words. "My company is very successful," he'd said, beaming, at the start of the meal, and he was still elaborating on his many outstanding qualities at the end. Over coffee (one for each of us; the crispy duck had put him in an expansive mood) there was a pause. "But enough about me," he said, his voice turning serious. "Let's talk about you. What did you want to interview me about?" I laughed—finally, a sense of humor. He looked perplexed.

Late in the second week, my mood continued to sour when my divorce notice arrived in the mail, on the eve of what would have been my sixth wedding anniversary. The timing and abruptness were striking. But though I'd assumed that the finality of the divorce would hit like a sock in the jaw, it didn't. When the paper arrived, I read it once, folded it, and put it away. While the document left me unhappy, it didn't sink me into despair. Nothing had, actually, since the weird night before my birthday. Which was fortunate, since the rumblings I'd been feeling from a place deep below were becoming an insistent growl, a roar that was moving up close, to the surface.

GONE

IN FEBRUARY, WHEN MY INSURANCE KICKED IN, I CALLED
Altman. I didn't wait to hear what he had to say. "It's still there,"
I said. "I want you to send me to see someone who will do something about this. Now." He gave me the name of a breast surgeon. I made an appointment to see him in his office.

Walter Victor was tall and compact, with a long, elegant face.
He wore a neatly pressed gray suit. He had on a wafer-thin gold
watch. He wasn't concerned by what he saw. "I don't think it's
anything," he said, peering at my breast. "It looks like a cyst to
me. If you want me to check, I can aspirate—stick a small needle
in and if fluid comes out, it's a cyst." I wanted him to. He had to
push to get the needle in. The lump was hard, resistant. I looked
down. There was no fluid coming out of my breast, only a thin
metal thread.

"I still don't think this is anything," he said. "It's probably a
fibroid. I see dozens of these every week. They only rarely turn
out to be something."

"Like plane crashes?" I said, trying to keep my anger down. I
thought of all the magazine articles I'd read about breast
cancer. They made it sound like doctors were standing by anx-
iously awaiting your call if you found any kind of thicken-
ing. Don't wait, they exhorted. In the stories, it was always
the women who wouldn't do their part, who were reluctant to

examine themselves or go for mammograms. The articles never said what might happen to these women, so fainthearted they couldn't touch their own breasts, if they had to face the demands of chemotherapy. One might conclude they'd be scared to death within five days anyway, so what difference would a preemptive exam make?

Nor did the stories explore the scenario I now found myself in. What was a patient supposed to do if her doctors kept blowing her off?

If it had been ten years later, I could probably have found easy counsel. But this was before breast cancer activism and awareness months, before pink ribbons and Susan Love's *Breast Book* and the boom in support groups. Celebrities still kept a lid on it when they got sick. As far as public figures who'd had breast cancer went, there were the two Bettys, Rollins and Ford, and that was about it. In 1989 the disease was a disease, not a cause, and I was thirty-three, too young to know anyone who'd had it. Lynn, my best friend from college, had contracted a brain tumor eight years after graduation, but her blasting headaches, the radioactive rods they'd implanted in her head—well, that was nothing like this. I hoped.

If I'd been, say, forty-three, I might have received the flood of letters that often follow a breast cancer diagnosis, the written offers of support from women who've had the disease, or have had a close friend who did. But people my age were still getting the hang of thank-you notes. If they were like me, they weren't even aware that anyone sent cancer notes, much less what sentiments were expressed. I was surprised to receive the one letter I did get, from a former coworker named Bob, who confided that he'd had testicular cancer but was fine now and hoped that I would be, too.

Not knowing Bob well, I didn't call and ask if he'd had to strong-arm his doctors into action when he'd found his lump. Anyway, my guess was he hadn't.

"What I usually tell women with these is just to go home and not worry," Victor was saying, with a shake of his head and a little chuckle. *Those jittery girls!* "But if you really want me to, if you need it for your peace of mind, I can biopsy it."

Biopsy it, I said in a low, hard voice, and his smile flattened. All right, he said, leaning back. All right, if I wanted him to. In later years, I've reflected on what would have become of me if I'd had a more timid disposition, if I'd been more like one of those squeamish women in the stories. But I don't have to wonder about this for very long. The answer's clear. I would be dead.

Any filmmaker looking for a surreally charged scene could do worse than a breast biopsy. The patient is brought into the sterile, green-tinged operating theater, settled on the table, and asked to lower her gown, after which one arm is tied down so she can't jerk or struggle, an orderly explains. The patient flinches once when the cold lidocaine is applied, more from anticipation than sensation. She flinches again, for real, when the anesthesia needle goes in, one sting, then two, then four and five. There's nothing to watch, to distract her from the uncomfortable tugs below, so she gazes up at the huge fly-eye lamp overhead, then settles on the surgeon's brown eyes, which appear relaxed in their focus.

And then they're not. The patient's drifted off, just for an instant, but a suspension of movement pulls her attention back to the eyes, which have suddenly, remarkably widened. The doctor's leaning closer, tensed. There's no question he's seen something. There's no question now. He knows.

I was still getting dressed when Victor started banging on the changing room door. "When you come out, I need to talk to you," he called. Even muffled, his voice carried a pulse of adrenaline. So this was it, I thought, slipping into mind-jam. I knew that when I left the room, I would be walking into a diagnosis of cancer, but oddly, fear wasn't paralyzing, or even touching, me, in any way I could detect. I experienced only a brief surge of relief—

thank God someone was finally paying attention—followed by a prick of annoyance. I'd had to wait all this time. He could wait five minutes while I figured out how to get my sweater on without making the stitches pull.

Out in the hall, I became like the Shona in Zimbabwe, who, lacking a word for cancer, are unable to receive diagnoses, to the frustration of their Western doctors. "I found a malignancy," Victor was explaining as we sat side by side on a bench outside the OR. The woman seated beside us turned her head away. A malignancy? But I'd thought I had breast cancer.

Contrapuntal thinking was beyond me. My mind could only run on one narrow track at a time. He kept talking on. The place where my stitches were hurt. Finally he was quiet. I made an appointment to see him again, then went downstairs to find the friend who'd come with me.

"I have a malignancy," I told her. She stopped fumbling with her coat, stared at me, nodded slowly. It was bad.

"A malignancy," I yelled over rush-hour traffic on a pay phone call to my mother. The telephone in the sublet wasn't working. It would take calls, wouldn't dial out. "A malignancy," I shouted on the street corner as people hurried past. "That's what he said. Don't tell anyone." I wanted time to think before word got around. I didn't want anyone calling up. I didn't want to talk about it. If I had to, it could become real.

Upstairs, the phone rang. It was my cousin Cia in Denver. "I just want you to know," she said, "I have my church group praying for you."

"What?" I said. I was furious. Oh shit, I thought. Struggling into my coat again, I got back into the elevator and pressed 1.

"You told Cia," I yelled into the corner phone. It was nearly seven P.M. now. The streets were darker, and emptier.

"No, I didn't," my mother said.

"Yes, you did! She just called! She knows!"

"No, I told your sister. *She* must have told Cia," she said, trying to exempt herself on a technicality.

"But that's exactly what I didn't want to happen," I said. "Now everybody will know."

"I've told you what your brother says," she said, sounding hurt. "If you don't want the whole world to know, don't tell me." Lord—just once, couldn't she have kept gossip to herself? I hadn't yet learned the most basic cancer principle—that, initially, it acts as an intensifier. Outside of the movies, people aren't magically transformed or ennobled by it overnight. They just behave like more concentrated versions of themselves. For better. For worse.

"But I don't want to become a poster child for breast cancer," I said, ignoring the fact that no one was actually extending me this honor. The more concentrated version of me that emerged after the first diagnosis was a bit on the narcissistic side. Years later, some of both my mother's and my more unattractive traits would get sandblasted down, as another, more advanced cancer principle came into play—namely, that a concentration of force can produce change, but only over time. My mother and I would both have to smack up against mortality more than once before we were even slightly refigured.

"Call Diego," she added now. "When he didn't hear from you after the biopsy, he's been calling here frantic." Frightened, I'd alerted him to what was going on. I hung up and dialed him, got his machine.

Half an hour later, he phoned back and I repeated the diagnosis. Malignancy. Diego was subdued and sweet, gentle in a way I hadn't known him before. Damn. This *was* really bad.

Over the next few days, I confided in a few friends, and in my new boss. I asked him not to tell anyone. A plan was forming in my mind, a plan of avoidance. Maybe, if I kept the circle tight, I could keep this thing a secret. If hardly anyone knew, couldn't it be like it never happened? But when I met with Victor to discuss possible courses of treatment, none subtle, it became clear I'd have a better chance of hiding an elephant in the sublet than in letting the breast cancer go undetected.

I don't remember exactly when this news sunk in (although I'm certain it wasn't in therapy; we were still busy with those childhood issues). But I do recall the wire of fear that ran through me at Victor's mention of "a possible mastectomy." Unless you're in the third grade, you can't mistake the word *mastectomy* for anything else. My immediate response was bent. I'm not doing that, I thought. I can't. I have to go on dates. By then I'd begun to short-circuit. I sat in his office, watching him draw dotted circles that were meant to be breasts but which looked like targets, and wondered, How am I supposed to get a boyfriend if I only have one breast?

Victor was drawing diagrams because we'd arrived at an impasse. He couldn't express himself in comprehensible English. I couldn't have understood him if he had. I kept making him repeat phrases like "infiltrative ductal carcinoma," then going blank. Smokey Robinson, looping through my head, was filling in the white places. "But in the case of carcinoma in situ," Victor would say before his voice faded out and Smokey's falsetto swelled up. *Baby, let's cruise . . . away from here. Don't be confused. The way is clear.* I didn't know you were supposed to take someone along to write everything down for you to study afterward. Instead I'd brought a Walkman, which I'd kept clamped to my head in the reception area. In the waiting room, the slumped, frail people scared me. Across from me, one old man, yellow, with drifty eyes, sat stick straight, as if on his best behavior. I pushed up the volume. *Let the music take your mind. Just release and you will find . . .*

The idea that music is a curative force has been around forever. The Greeks thought it had the power to heal the body and soul. The Egyptians prescribed incantations for the sick. Nowadays hospitals experiment with broadcasting Bach in the OR, as researchers have determined that, among its other benefits, music can boost endorphin levels, lower anxiety, diminish a patient's need for painkillers, even juice the immune system by causing the body to increase production of immunoglobulin A and interleukin-1. Perhaps all this explains what one weird study conducted in Finland found, that cancer patients who attend cultural events live longer than those who don't.

Rhythm is inherently connected to survival. I once read an essay by a man who went down in a plane crash and, stranded in the wilderness with a broken leg, slowly rocked himself to safety. Rhythm has the effect of activating the right hemisphere of the brain, the side that governs feelings, dreams, the unconscious, the side I was beginning to draw on in my meetings with Victor.

The first time music caught me was in sixth grade. I was sitting in the car, waiting for my mother to return from the grocery store, when the Supremes' "Baby Love" came on the radio, and I was gone. The word *caught*, in Argentine slang, has sexual overtones, and that's exactly how the song affected me. Even at eleven, I had a hazy sense that this was fuck music. I wanted more.

Music steadied me through high school. When I was sixteen and stalled in depression, I painted the walls of my room deep purple, wrote melodramatic song lyrics along the base. *If I could choose a place to die, it would be in your arms* was the motto closest to the bed. I wasn't sure whose arms Eric Clapton or I were referring to, just that his sentiments matched mine. My parents were forced to confront the purple mood chamber every time they went upstairs.

Like everyone my age, I thought I was listening to revolutionary anthems. I would have been horrified to be told it, but the music was also our religious hymns, our spirituals. Jimi Hendrix and Johnny Winter took us to a higher plane, even if the spirits that moved us were of the lower variety. The sanctity may have been chemically induced, but it held the promise of divinity all the same.

It's no surprise, then, that waiting in Victor's office, desperately in need of grace, I took up again with Motown. Labile, skidding along the continuum between Eros and Thanatos, I was trying to push myself in the direction away from death. I was sending my body the signal: Please live.

". . . prognosis is excellent." Victor was weighing my options, which amounted to two. I could have a lumpectomy, in which case he would excise the lump, leaving the breast intact, then send me for chemotherapy and radiation, to wipe out any cancer that might be left. In 1989 chemo was just becoming standard follow-up treatment for all young women who had lumpectomies, regardless of whether their lymph nodes indicated the beginnings of spread or not. With women under thirty-five, treatment is more aggressive because their breast cancer tends to be more aggressive, more likely to recur and to be fatal. ("Young women with early stage breast cancer do significantly worse when compared to older women in terms of relapse-free survival, cause-specific survival, distant metastasis and breast and regional node recurrence," a study at the University of Pennsylvania determined in 1994.)

My other choice, a mastectomy, meant that though I'd lose the breast, I could skip the chemo and keep the hair.

At some point in the discussion, Victor must have mentioned reconstruction, but if he did, it wasn't at length. I don't remember comprehending that I could have my breast rebuilt. Nor did he explain that I had time to think about all this—that if it had taken the lump seven years to grow, inaction for another week or so wasn't going to make a big difference. Instead he began edging the talk around to a decision.

"Statistically speaking, the outcome with mastectomies is about the same as with lumpectomies," he said, pencil poised. But we'd run out of possibilities to diagram.

"So what do I do?" I asked.

"I can't tell you," he said. It was the clearest sentence he'd said since we sat down. The man talked like someone who'd been walled up in a medical compound for the last twenty years. Once, when he asked for the name of my drugstore, the Chateau pharmacy, he'd said, puzzled, "Chateau? Like a steak?" He spoke in med wonk. "What *is* a lymph node dissection?" I'd ask, and he'd answer: A lymph node dissection is, um, it is a lymph node dissection, a dissection of the lymph nodes. Performed under general anesthesia, he added, as if to elucidate.

Now we were at another impasse. He couldn't tell me what I should do. I couldn't understand enough of what he had said to be able to make up my mind. My instincts told me to get up and walk out, find someone who could make himself understood. But I still hadn't learned how to fight for my life. I still hadn't seen that my instincts could be trusted, that they were platinum, transponders, that they were what would, in fact, get me through.

I ignored the counsel from my right brain and, instead, tried again.

"Really, I don't know," I said. "You have to tell me: What do you think?"

"Even old ladies want to keep their breasts," he said, somewhat inscrutably. "I had one who was seventy-nine and she didn't want a mastectomy. She wouldn't let me." He smiled at this remembered feistiness, then continued. "I guess I'd say the lumpectomy," he said. "Considering your age and your circumstances." My single state. "With six months' chemotherapy."

"Okay, the lumpectomy," I agreed. He told me his secretary would make the necessary hospital arrangements. Inexperienced as I was, I didn't think to ask if the hospital was known for its oncology department. In fact, it wasn't. Instead I folded up the drawings and reached for my purse. The Walkman was clipped to the strap. I didn't need to press the "on" button. I was already in rewind.

Even though I was expecting it, the blast, when it came, side-swiped me, shred me, it flung me into a parched, strange land. When I was able to stand again and survey my surroundings, I couldn't tell where I was. Some landmarks still existed—the buildings I passed each day, the physical geography of the city—but they weren't the same, as if they'd been blown off course with me. If they weren't where they'd been, were they even land-marks? The city had shifted. So had selves within; I wasn't sure which of these was true anymore. I was hungry to set everything back as it was. I didn't care if everything had been lousy. I might have howled for familiarity, if it would have helped. I could have howled, too, if I'd wanted, for back then in Cancerland, I was alone in a way that was absolute, foul.

As if on its own momentum, my other life continued to unfold. I could almost believe I was making the promising new start I'd anticipated. I met with agents. I took authors out. I had one lunch with a hip, funny magician to see if he wanted to write about his partner. I had another, at my boss's request, with an aging starlet to learn if she'd divulge details on what Warren Beatty had been like in bed. ("I don't remember," she said over sushi. "I was too drunk at the time. But," she added brightly, "I'm in AA now!")

I bought a nightgown for the hospital. I left work early to look at scarves. I phoned Victor with questions I'd forgotten to ask. How soon after the operation would I be able to start working out again? "As far as I'm concerned," he said, "you can bring running shoes to the hospital and do laps around the corridor." I canceled lunch plans for two weeks down the line with the excuse that I'd be out of town.

I was adjusting to the culture shock of being in a new country, one charted by Susan Sontag and Anatole Broyard and other writers I hadn't yet read. In Cancerland, I was just beginning to learn, people are forced to live in two time zones at once. We exist on cancer's time and real-world time simultaneously. We continue to care about our love lives and careers and vacations and retirement plans—about the big and the small—but with a particular urgency, since the clock is racing, double time. This double time magnifies all our emotions: Compassion and sorrow. Fear and relief. Irritation and joy—the first, because each day has to be redemption; the second, because each day is.

On the eve of a friend's wedding, I stayed over at her apartment to help keep her nerves calm. We played a board game from sixth grade called Mystery Date and I won Allan, the cute one. "Lucky in Mystery Date, unlucky in love," I said. We were giddy and self-consciously girly the whole night. It made perfect sense to me to be thirty-three and having a pretend slumber party. Why not? I was having a pretend life.

I didn't say anything to my friend about the cancer. I didn't want to cast a pall on the ceremony. Through repetition, it was getting easier to keep the secret, but it was also getting harder, in practical ways. The morning after I let him know the date of my lumpectomy, my new boss stopped by my office.

"Look, I can't tell you what to do," he said. "But I think you should tell people what's going on. People around here are starting to notice you're out a lot. They're starting to talk. If you don't say something, they could think it's much worse."

Worse than cancer? I thought.

"If you don't say something," he cautioned, "they're going to think I hired a flake."

Everyone was going to find out soon enough, I figured. I went ahead and told a couple of people. It was awkward—I didn't know anyone well—so I stopped at two and let the office grapevine take care of the rest. In one respect, it was a good thing the editor pushed me into outing myself when he did. "Did you get a second opinion?" the managing editor asked. "I think you have to or the insurance company won't pay." Oh, hell. I hadn't. The operation was three days away. I rushed to find another doctor.

"Damn it," Victor said when I called to ask if he could suggest someone. "They want *what?* Oh, Jesus Christ. I had one woman call her nutritionist and the nutritionist told her not to go ahead." He sighed.

"Um, it's not me. It's the insurance company," I said. I'd had a sense he wasn't going to like having his judgment questioned. "They're making me," I said, hoping to appease him. Not having visited many doctors, I didn't see that his response was extreme. But now I think: Why shouldn't I have gotten a second opinion? Or a third or fourth or fifth? Medicine has shifted into the strictly quantifiable realm—more and more, decisions about who qualifies for a procedure, about how long a hospital stay can be, are made on a pure cost-pricing basis. Patient A is over fifty-five? Sorry; in that case the odds with operation B are too small to make sound financial sense. I still hadn't learned that, to get the best care, I had to behave like a consumer. I should have told myself: Someone is going to be getting big bucks to perform this lumpectomy. May the best doctor win this account. And I should have shopped around, the way I would have if I were buying, say, a computer. Instead I allowed myself to be railroaded by ego.

"All right," he said. "If you have to. My secretary will give you a name."

The other doctor was a gynecologist. He didn't question the plans.

Altman sounded frightened when I called to let him know what was going on. "What?" he said. "Did you ever tell me about this lump?" I thought I heard papers rustling in the background.

"Yeah. I did," I said coldly.

"Oh." The rustling stopped. "There's something here."

He'd been so unconcerned before, I could only imagine he was afraid for his insurance rates.

"Don't worry, I'm not going to sue you," I said, as condescendingly as I could. Let him see how it felt. "I just wanted you to know." I wasn't out for blood. The man hadn't chopped off a wrong leg or prescribed maiming doses of a drug. He was guilty, maybe, of negligence—and, no question, of behaving like a goofball. I had enough on my hands without taking on a lengthy lawsuit. Mainly, I was filling him in because I wanted to be sure that the next time a woman called, scared because she'd found a lump, he'd think twice before dismissing her.

We talked about Victor. I mentioned he'd sent me to see the gynecologist.

"He's a nice guy," Altman said. "Too bad he's losing his license."

"What?" I said.

"Yeah. It's too bad," he said. "He's the guy who gave Joel Steinberg that baby."

Victor had sent me to the person who'd illegally placed Lisa Steinberg with the man who tortured and killed her. The cancer was horrifying. These doctors were beginning to seem horrifying, too. In figuring out how the medical system worked, I was learning that one of the most important things was to distrust it.

"The reason I stay in New York is there are more doctors here to fire," a woman who'd had cancer later told me. But at that point, I still didn't understand that if you wanted, for any reason, you could just fire your doctor. With the operation bearing down, so close, I probably wouldn't have had the strength anyway.

The afternoon before the lumpectomy, I checked into the hospital. My mother waited with me in the admitting room. I kept my Walkman on and wouldn't talk. In the room, she and Diego were distraction until visiting hours were over. Afterward my roommate pulled the curtain back. She was not much older than

I was, but the set of her mouth made her look matronly, or maybe it was the fact that her unwashed brown hair was stringy and flat. Groaning, she shifted out of her bed and plodded over to the foot of mine. She'd just had a mastectomy, she said, leaning on the metal frame. I couldn't help it. I glanced at her chest. The outline of one pendulous breast was obvious; the other side of the nightgown hung straight. And me? What was I in for? Who was that who'd come by: My mother? My boyfriend? Briefly, I recounted my story. When I got to the part about the divorce, she shook her head. "Thank God I have a husband," she said, and I wondered what new kinds of vexation fate was planning to spring on me.

The lumpectomy was scheduled for nine A.M. At nine-thirty, my mother and I were still waiting. A few minutes before ten, Victor rushed into the room. He was still in street clothes, in a brown suit. He was holding tight to a file, as if it were an anchoring weight. I could see he was jittery. His nerves unnerved me. He'd just had a look at my slides, he said. It appeared I had a second problem.

"I've just noticed that you also have carcinoma in situ," he said. "This argues more strongly for a mastectomy." Carcinoma in situ, he'd explained when we met, was possible embryonic disease—abnormal cells that develop, 20 percent of the time, into invasive cancer.

Years later a friend discovered she had carcinoma in situ. It took her two weeks to decide what to do. The condition alone isn't exceptionally dangerous. She might have lived with it. But because her mother had had breast cancer, she didn't want to take the risk. Eventually she chose to have a double mastectomy. In deciding, she consulted various doctors. She read numerous books. She was able to weigh her options, in part because she did not have a fidgety surgeon standing by her bed. Mastectomy? Or not? This one wanted to know, and now.

Precise calculations were essential, I told myself—think hard—but my mind was snowy. The only complete thought I could form was: He's just now looking at the slides? I remembered the roommate's one sad, dangling breast. "Do I have to?" I asked.

Victor twisted his mouth. "No," he said, exhaling. "No, I guess you could still have the lumpectomy."

"Did you discover this on the mammogram?" my mother asked.

"Actually, I didn't do a mammogram," he said.

"What?" my mother said. "You're taking her in now and you neglected to do a mammogram? I'm sorry. She's not going anywhere until you do."

"But I can't," he said. "The operating room is booked. They're waiting. It's reserved."

"You have to," my mother said. "I'm sorry. You have to."

"All right," he said, grinning as if he'd been naughty. "Let me see what I can do."

He hurried out. My mother was talking, but I couldn't hear her. I was tumbling, falling between time zones into the place where there is no dimension. I was cruising through an imploded land, skimming a country that has no spaces, only invisible planes.

Ten minutes later, Victor returned, smiling. "Come on," he said buoyantly, as if we were all joining in a triumph that we'd planned for some time. "Come on, Kathy. We're going for the mammogram."

He waited. I began looking for my shoes.

We were going down.

FLASH

THE NEXT AFTERNOON, I WAS ON THE PHONE. "I'M SORRY,
we don't visit lumpectomies," the woman at the other end was
saying. The telephone was on a table to my left. I was thickly
bandaged on the same side. It had taken a tricky, sideways reach
to place the call.

"But my doctor said you would be the ones to show me what
to do," I replied. "He said I should call you." There were arm
exercises I was supposed to be doing, to restore mobility. Her
organization was in the business of demonstrating them. Or had
been.

"I'm afraid we've had cutbacks," the woman said. "We don't
have the staff. We can only come by if you're a mastectomy."

Twisting gingerly, I hung up. Obviously, lumpectomies were
considered spry, but if that was true, I couldn't imagine what
shape the mastectomies were in. Though after surgery I'd been
surprised to find I wasn't in strong pain ("There aren't a lot of
nerve endings in the breasts," Victor had explained), I'd been
unhappy to discover my left arm was heavy, useless. With Vulcan
concentration, I could raise it an inch.

The lymph node dissection, not the lumpectomy, is what had
caused this impairment. Breast cancer travels through the lymph
system, so after slicing out the tumor, Victor had cut a thin line
across my underarm and removed—dissected—a string of lymph

glands to check for the disease. A count of zero positive nodes was, of course, best; 1 to 3 was not ideal; and 4 to 10 wasn't good. Over 10, and they'd begin an immediate watch for metastases, spread, to the liver, lungs, brain, bone—the outlying territories that advancing breast cancer most often invades.

(Node dissections are far from an exact science. Not only are they fuzzy predictors—30 percent with negative nodes go on to develop metastases all the same—they're potentially disfiguring. Thirty percent of women who have them eventually develop a condition called lymphodema, in which the arm and hand become permanently swollen, sometimes to elephantine size. Lymph glands are conduits for lymph fluid. They exist to move fluid along. But if the glands are removed, fluid can pool in the forearm, say, and stagnate there. A much less destructive procedure, involving radioactive dye, has been around for some time, and while it would virtually eliminate lymphodema, hardly any doctors are using it. "You know surgeons," breast surgeon Susan Love said at a conference a few years ago, when asked why it wasn't more commonplace. "They like to do things the way they've always done them.")

"The report on your nodes was good," my surgeon said on his first bedside visit. "You had zero. Maybe one. The lab's not sure."

Not sure?

"They can't tell. Some of the tumor could have gotten mixed in with the nodes."

Nice work. But my spirits, if not my confidence in the lab, were lifted by the news. I might have been less elated had I known that even one node is cause for serious concern: Half of all women with only one node positive have a recurrence anyway, and most in that group die of the disease.

I told him I needed him to teach me the arm exercises. "The organization you wanted me to call won't send anyone," I said.

Victor made a face. "I don't know them," he said. "That group are the ones that are supposed to teach you." This was my first experience with the splintering of care that's common outside cancer centers—with the way patients are shuttled among specialists, none of whom will come forward and take charge.

"How am I supposed to learn?" I asked.

"I don't know. Maybe I can remember. There's one that's like the inky-dinky spider," he said, his hand frolicking up an invisible garden spout. I tried the same move. My spider was seized by death throes on the ground.

"Isn't there an easier exercise?" I asked. Victor frowned. The inky-dinky hand walk was the only one he knew.

I think I was in the hospital three days. I can't be sure. My memories of the lumpectomy aren't linear. When I try to reproduce them, they come back jumbled, embedded in the sense panels that are created by trauma.

"The mind doesn't process trauma in the same way," a friend who's a shrink says on the subject of post-traumatic stress syndrome. "The memories are different from normal ones. They're more cinematic—when someone tries to remember, they're flooded with the experience, like it's happening all over again. That's why you hear about flashbacks, about Vietnam vets hitting the ground when a car backfires. People walk around in the memory, as if it's really going on."

If an event is too painful for comprehension, it may remain in a container the mind constructs to keep it at a safe remove. Never having been fully absorbed, it continues to exert a half-life force, to wield a sickly, intrusive power. Trauma is a vampire, but light, as any student of folklore or Freud knows, will kill it. The problem is, when the shell-shocked try to exhume their memories—to bring them into the light—the result can be a death struggle so fierce, they may fear it's them, not the suckling pain, that's about to die.

My memories of the lumpectomy have been shuffled and respliced. A few are still locked away.

In one murky sequence, Altman stops by. From her chair, my mother glares. I've told her what happened. "Anything you want," he says, laughing too hard, when I say I'm upset and want a sedative. Fade, I'm alone, and fade once more. My mother is back. "Where's Dr. Feelgood?" she asks, a reference both to his gladly-fondle-you remark and to the Valiums I've cadged.

Images of flowers, of well-wishers, resurface in Technicolor: Most everyone who comes brings the toys from their childhood sickroom, a gesture of maternal concern, an invitation to regression. David, an army of green plastic soldiers. Robin, a copy of *Curious George*. Judy, pink socks with frilly lace; a good-luck candle; a smooth, carved-stone bird from Nicaragua that fits perfectly in the palm of my hand. Alone, I get comfort from squeezing it.

The starlet who can't remember her lovers sends an arrangement of tiger lilies and tulips.

In some frames, the focus is skewed. A man is in a plastic chair by my bed. He's someone I've gone out with occasionally, every month or so, for half a year. Memory has eroded his features—his nose was long and sharp, I think—but the fabric swatches he brought remain clear. He's arranging them across my blanketed knees to illustrate his decorator's plans.

"Your cousin told you I was here?" I say, stroking a bit of brocade. I haven't told him what I'm in for, but he's a doctor. He must have asked the nurses at the front desk.

"Yeah, Meryl called," he says. "You're having a minor procedure?"

"It's breast cancer," I blurt out, not having rehearsed a cover story. As my face reddens, I think: Calm down. The man's a doctor. He'll understand.

"Oh, no. Oh, you're kidding. Oh, my God, I'm so sorry," he says, his voice squeaking before dropping into the sympathy range. From the way he quickly scoops up the swatches, I know I'll never hear from him again.

Isn't he embarrassed not to call? I wondered afterward, until I realized: Better that he made a quick break than got involved out of guilt. Eight months earlier, the melodrama of the story would have had a perverse appeal—I got breast cancer and a man dropped me! But I was learning to resist the impulse toward mawkishness. It seemed dangerous to play at being a victim when reality was intruding so uncomfortably on that role.

One other scene, in the hospital lounge: I'm in a gown, on a couch, leaning toward a new doctor, an oncologist whose name is William Bonner. He looks friendly and unflappable, a suburban dad, a dark-haired Barney Rubble. I listen as he details his plan for treatment: six months of chemotherapy in three-week cycles, then six weeks of radiation. The chemo will be CAF, acronym for a trio of drugs—Cytoxan, Adriamycin, and 5FU. "5FU?" I say, laughing. My feelings exactly. I'll go to his nearby office for injections, which will take about three hours and will cause, he's sure I know, a few side effects. I brace for elaboration. He dodges.

"Chemotherapy works by attacking fast-growing cells," he says. "It kills not just the cancer, but every fast-growing cell in the body. Cells in the stomach lining are fast growing. That's why you can get nausea. So are the cells in your nails. And in your hair follicles."

He hasn't said, so I ask. "Am I going to lose my hair?"

He rotates one shoulder casually, like a person who's spent too long in the gym. "In the majority of cases, with Adriamycin, patients may experience substantial hair loss."

"But am I going to lose it?" If I have to do this, he can't hide behind brochure language.

"Probably," he says. "Yes."

"Really, that's fine with me," I bluff. "I don't care. I pierced my nose when I was nineteen and I was planning to shave my head, too. Now I can see what it looks like." As if the man cares about my credentials of cool. As if, by acting tough, I'll ice him with the message: Don't fuck with me. But that's exactly why he's here—

to fuck with me, down to my DNA—exactly how he's figuring on giving me his best shot, so to speak.

Chemotherapy can be tough, the oncologist concedes, but with it, my odds are 85 percent, assuming the one node was positive. Eighty-five percent sounds like a comforting figure, until I do a little digging and learn it's not quite the survival vote it seems. Yes, five years after treatment, 85 percent of patients with my diagnosis are still alive. But five years is a misleading date. And 85 percent is a misleading number. With some cancers, if you're clean for five years, you're considered cured, but not with breast cancer, which tends to grow more slowly than other types and therefore takes longer to reappear. Figure the odds within a more meaningful time frame—at, say, seven years, when breast cancer is more likely to have recurred—and things look a little darker.

Besides, 85 percent doesn't mean 85 percent cured. It's a head count of everyone who hasn't died. It doesn't distinguish between the people who are well and the ones who've relapsed and are back on chemo, or are pleading for entry into an experimental drug program, or are trying their luck—rotten so far, but who knows?—in one of those shady Mexican towns where cure peddlers tell stories that will make a woman's heart leap. At least for a while.

Any questions? the oncologist asks.

A couple. Has he ever seen an allergic reaction to chemo? Because I've got a psycho immune system, hair-triggered and whacked, that stages stealth attacks on foreign substances. Once, when I was a kid, a dip in a brackish pond caused my throat to close, and my mother had to rush me to the pediatrician we saw in cases of emergency. By this point, my mother had thrown in the towel with Christian Science, although she remained a devout medical skeptic.

And once, as an adult, I was nearly flat-lined by an allergic reaction to medicine. Getting dressed for work, I took a couple of Anaprox for a headache, and within seconds, my tongue had turned as black as a hanged man's; my blood pressure was plummeting. Anaphylactic shock, the paramedics who burst into the apartment said, and had traffic stalled the ambulance even ten minutes more, it would have killed me.

If my immune system can go berserk over pond scum, I can't imagine what it's going to do with chemotherapy. Bonner isn't worried. He says he's never seen a life-threatening allergy to chemo.

The standard reactions, I'll discover later, are bad enough.

One other question. If I have cancer, why aren't I in pain?

"Pain only happens at the end, when someone's much sicker," he says.

But that's not true, I think. Right from the beginning, Lynn was in pain. I'm tempted to ask him about that, but I can't think how to talk about her. Lynn, my college roommate, was my cohort on one summer-long boy-crazed stampede through Europe and my best friend for a few years after, till she married and we moved apart. Lynn was ebullient: kind and wild at heart. Of her many attributes, at nineteen, I most admired her gutter mouth. "The harder they come, the further they shoot" was one of her finer sophomore-year cracks.

She'd gotten sick with a brain tumor at thirty, two months before she was going to get married for the second time. Since I've been diagnosed, she's been continually on my mind. With the oncologist here, I want to ask if it isn't strange for best friends from college to contract cancer, both, improbably young, just a decade on. Doesn't he think there was something in the earth, or in the cafeteria, or in the great lakes around Syracuse, where we went to school? Or, maybe, was it something we did? But I don't. I don't want to start thinking about how Lynn looked when she traveled from Ohio to see me, five months after the wedding she'd hastily pulled together, six months after she'd been woken from a nap by what she described as the worst headache of her life. Badly blond in a cheap wig, bloated and red in a way that made me think, guiltily, of a hot dog, she was disoriented during the visit, confusing words and events. "I have money. We can take a bus," she said, meaning cab. And "Why does he have to be here?" she said, looking grumpily at poor Diego, who pretended to read the newspaper across the living room. "Because he's my husband. We're married," I explained, and she answered, "Oh."

When I remember the last time, what comes flooding back is not the love I felt for Lynn, but the cowardly way I shrank from her, disconcerted by her appearance. "I can't have lunch with you tomorrow," I lied as I smoothed a sheet over the futon. "I have a meeting. But you can leave your suitcase at my office." The next day at noon, the receptionist rang: "Lynn Grossman is here for lunch." Annoyed, I came out and repeated the lie. "Lynn. I told you. I can't. I'm busy." "But my plane is delayed," she sighed. "I hate when they do that," she added, and that was all we said.

I shouldn't have been surprised when her sister called a few weeks later. It's a measure of how thick my shell had grown that the news, in fact, broadsided me. But Lynn had *sworn* the doctors said she would be okay, I protested. But she'd just come to see me on a business trip, I said, as the realization sunk in that, really, she'd come to say good-bye and I'd behaved like an absolute jerk. Once I understood what had happened, what I'd done, I don't know which hammered me harder, guilt or grief.

Three years later, shame still checks me. I try to mention her, but I can't. Bonner waits, and when there are no more questions, he stands, telling me where to call to make an appointment. "One suggestion," he adds. "Don't watch any of those made-for-TV movies. They wouldn't be a good idea."

That was all it took. What did the guy think, I was a baby? I was spoiling for a fight, cruising for a bruising, and I got one. Back in the sublet, I decided to prove my mettle. I went out and rented the big gun—*Bang the Drum Slowly*, a cheery little film that begins, "Actually, you get over it fairly quick. You might not think so, but it's true. You're driving along with a man who's been told he's dying, and yet everything keeps going on." By the time a stumbling Robert De Niro was groping his way into the dugout, I was a sobbing, hysterical wreck.

The film choice was lunacy. But it was also a catalyst. I'd been raised never to show emotion, even when I was by myself. The only time I saw my mother in tears, she'd been faking it. "What should I do?" she'd asked when, at twenty, I ratted to her about my sister's plans to run away with an exceptionally mangy boyfriend. "Cry," I advised her. "That'll startle her so much, she won't go." My mother's subsequent stirring performance did the trick. My sister was so astonished, she cashed in her bus ticket.

In my upbringing, tears were weakness, and I knew I was going to have to be strong. I wasn't acting stoic; I was stoic. I was determined to muscle through, not understanding that by stuffing the anguish, I was setting myself up for a fall. I found ways to block the fear. Two days out of the hospital, I began running again, though the pounding made the stitches sting. I went to work. I went out with friends. I went to therapy, where the Freudian was concentrating on how abandoned I must have felt at three, when my sister was born, and at seven, with the arrival of my brother. We were getting into the tough stuff, she said, though she never once asked about the cancer and I only brought it up in practical terms ("I have to change my time next week—I've got an appointment with the oncologist").

The worst times were at night, when anxiety would build and make me frantic, but then I'd have a few drinks and get muzzy. Mostly it worked. Once or twice, I was up all night, doing dawn patrol with the channel changer.

I would have been undone to have been told I was denying illness. Intellectually, I wasn't. I bought books on the subject. I read up. I was eager to know more about cancer. I just didn't want to know one thing—that I had it.

Reading became a way of distancing myself. I became versed in cancer patients, the way an anthropologist specializes in a tribe. These patients, I learned, were haunted by curious fears—that their bodies had sabotaged them, that they'd inadvertently brought on their own disease. More curious still was the way that paradox plagued them. The treatment for their illness, for instance, was often worse than the disease and might, on its own, cause new and different cancers. (No mention was made of how later, with luck, paradox turns into blessing. In the Buddhist view, human beings only begin to live after they've confronted death, which could account for why the dying and the newly recovering may say they've never felt more alive.) Even when they became well, I learned, they often lived in dread, for they were continually shadowed by the threat of recurrence. "Under a Damocles sword," the books always put it. Their emotional life was further complicated by the fact that their illness might repel other people, making them—although the books didn't quite say it so boldly—social outcasts. As the American Cancer Society's guide delicately advised, "Although you might appreciate their efforts, members of the square dance club, for example, may not feel comfortable visiting a casual acquaintance in the hospital." In other words, these patients should be prepared for some fast do-sie-dos.

This distance was easy to maintain, for while I found lots of advice in my reading, I encountered no examples of anyone like me. The women in the books might have jumped ship from *Good Housekeeping*. They were graying and settled, concerned more with families than with bosses or careers. They were Mary Worth with bum mammograms. None of them appeared to have been hoping for wild sex flings in the days leading up to their diagnoses. Few were even dating. I did find one article written by a single woman. "Cancer is an asshole detector," she observed, rather ominously, on the subject of men.

A friend gave me a book called *Love, Medicine & Miracles*, an examination of what the author, a doctor named Bernie Siegel, calls Exceptional Cancer Patients, or ECaPs. "More than 2 million copies sold," a banner on the cover proclaimed, McDonald's-style. After reading *Love*, I suspected that friends and relatives of the stricken, in need of a quick hospital gift, were largely to blame for sales. I haven't met many actual cancer patients who particularly liked the book. The ECaPs, for starters, are obnoxious can-do paragons. "While the typical patient may ask, 'Why me, Lord?'" Siegel writes, "the exceptional patient says . . . 'Try me, Lord.'" It's the reader's patience that's tried as Siegel, who shaves his head bald like a cancer sufferer in what might be construed as a PR move, serves up one glowing testimonial after the next—usually to himself. Nurses pop into patients' rooms and demand, "Tell me about Dr. Siegel." People whose tumors mysteriously shrink prior to chemotherapy don't credit their own efforts at, say, positive visualizations, but instead exclaim, "It must be that shiny-headed doctor."

Siegel was my introduction to a type: the self-appointed cancer guru. Cancer gurus are not lacking in ego. Early on in *Love*, Siegel arrives at this epiphany: Doctors are people, too. "We have all the problems other people have," he announces, obviously startled to discover this fact. Once clear on his own human stature, he decides to "get involved" with his patients, beginning by directing them to call him by his first name. "For the first time I began to understand fully what it's like to live with cancer, knowing the fear that it may be spreading," he writes, oblivious to the possibility that the verifiably sick might object to his use of the word *fully*. "How hard it is to keep one's integrity as a human being with this knowledge!" Guess what, Bern—millions of people, even children, have been managing it for years.

"That cancer-patient-as-hero myth turns me off," Laura, a woman who later became my meditation teacher, said in one of our discussions about the smarmy underside of New Age fervor. Laura and I share a history of cancer and a distaste for illness hype. "Don't get me started on the whole plucky-survivor thing. I hate all those stalwart women who show up in the women's magazines every October. And Siegel's people—they're beyond plucky."

Still, she conceded, "when I was really doing bad, I liked that all his examples were doing worse, and then they got better."

All right, I allow. *Love* wasn't a total wash for me either. One passage, titled "Why do you need this illness?," notes that "throughout our lives we've been trained to associate sickness with rewards," and encourages readers to ask themselves, essentially, what they're getting out of being sick. Stacks of insurance notices, I thought at first. But reflecting further, I saw how cancer was providing me with the first real opportunity to take it easy since college. Everyone I knew was career mad; so was I. But was that really the price of an exemption—a lethal illness? I wasn't sure if this was cause or effect, but I made a vow: From now on, I'd leave the office by six every day, no matter how unsettling the effort. Outside, the fading light of rush hour left me depressed. On the street, everyone else was hurrying home to bright apartments and families, while I was heading into an empty, sprawling evening. But I stuck to my resolve and even blew off an afternoon or two on the pretext of a doctor's appointment.

On one of those loose afternoons, I stopped by my neighborhood bookstore and made my way to the Health section. Flipping through a book about an actress who'd had a mastectomy, I came upon a description of how chemotherapy had made her vomit so hard, she'd cracked her head on the toilet seat and had to be taken to the hospital. *Cracked her head while throwing up*—what a double-strike loss of control. Woozy at the thought of it, I replaced the book on the shelf and hurried out. All night, I couldn't clear the image from my head.

———————

Even now, from a distance of ten years, my memories of the days connected to chemo can bring on actual nausea, a horrible, druggy stomach burn, insistent and severe as if the Adriamycin has just gone in three hours ago. All my memories of the first time are like that—vitrine, not celluloid, hard and jagged, shards. Whenever I've tried to return to them, to reach down into the container and bring them up, nausea surges through me, narrowing my attention, distracting it from thought into sensation. The phantom nausea's a warning—stay the hell away—and in the past, it's worked. I've fled, which is why, a decade on, the stench in the cask is still full-strength. There's been no air, no light, to fade the contents, so they've festered and grown; they've remained alive.

Cancer still has the power to make me retch. Cancer has a way of swelling on its own threat, for cancer likes to be a bully. But the disease has pummeled me one time too many. It's forced me down, smashed my head, it's nearly killed me. Then what's a little nausea? I think. By the end of my treatment, nausea was the least of it. So let the replay slash and burn, I'm not afraid anymore to turn and stare.

I'm not afraid now, at all.

PART TWO

HOW WE ARE MADE LIGHT

Pity the visitors
bent under shopping bags,
who have their huge hats
here where there are no seasons,
who run from station to station
with a question so inconsequential
even we patients smile.

admire the nurse and the aide
who fill out a form,
one beginning at the front,
the other at the end,
speaking of Bon Jovi;
the doctors, washing side by side,
discussing an even greater doctor;

most of all revere the orderlies
who have come from across the sea
to wheel us through the corridors
to a place where we will be tested
where we will finally belong
even more inherently than here,
where we will no longer be watchers
but the matter itself,
flesh and soul transposed
to degrees on a scale of radiance.

—D. Nurkse

HOPE

BONNER'S OFFICE WAS DRAB, LIKE A DENTIST'S. ON THE first day, a Friday, a friend met me there and stayed till they called my name. A nurse waited while she said good-bye, then the nurse brought me back. In the chemo room, they immediately put a blue ice bag on my head. It was supposed to prevent my hair from falling out by freezing the roots, but it proved to be useless and made me look like a fool. I sat in a reclining chair and the nurse worked the needle into my hand. It hurt. Then Bonner came in and started the IV drip. The first drug sent a chill up my arm and left a taste in my mouth like sauerkraut. The second drug, bright Kool Aid red, zapped my body with a violent buzz that warmed me horribly and made me squirm. "Adriamycin," he said. "It's called the red devil." Later, to myself, I called it Drano, or Agent Orange, for that's what it felt like rushing through my veins. My poor veins, I thought when I found out that Adriamycin is so corrosive, they have to be careful not to spill any on your skin or you could get third-degree burns and need skin grafts.

The first time, I didn't throw up, but you don't usually, not immediately. Chemo is cumulative. It takes a while. The first time, I slept twenty hours afterward. Bonner hadn't told me he'd added knockout drugs to the mix, and the resulting zombie state scared me some because I didn't know what was making me slur my words, what was clogging my movements. Once I got home,

Diego came up and stayed till I fell asleep. The next afternoon, when I awoke, he was gone.

The grogginess didn't last. But the sauerkraut taste wouldn't go away, and after a while, it deepened into a hard metallic tang. Everything I ate, everything I smelled, was rancid. I began to eat compulsively anyway, at first to try to get the taste out of my mouth, later, to blanket nausea.

In the week after chemo, I experienced two jolts. The first occurred when I went to church on Sunday. As an adult, I'd made occasional lunges at sanctity, but now that I had cancer, I thought I should get serious. So even though my legs were still wobbly, I put on a dress and went to an eleven o'clock service. I was fine, distracted by the proceedings, till the part that's called the peace, where the congregants turn and greet one another. When the man behind me clasped my hand, a wincing pain made me yank it back. Looking down, I saw it had aged forty years. The veins had raised into a knotty, black ganglia, like an old woman's, or a witch's. I quickly hid it against my thigh.

The words of the service were empty that day. But I hadn't found meaning in church for years. I left before Communion, drawn out by the late-March air that was fast warming into spring. Walking toward the river, I tried cobbling together prayers in my head, but I didn't know whom I was talking to. The God of my childhood had stopped making sense years before. In college, as a religion major, I'd studied what one professor had called the God of the Gaps, but that was just a vague, academic's deity who didn't do much besides tiptoe around existential holes in logic. I felt silly addressing an intellectual construct. What I needed was a God of action. In Riverside Park, long stretches of new grass looked soft, like the air. A community garden was blooming in a riot of disarray. Bending down to check again whether tulips have scent, I caught myself: A cancer patient stopping to smell the flowers? *How embarrassing.* But earth laughs in flowers, Emerson said, and I was getting exactly what I needed:

some laughter. Even if I didn't know it. Even if I'd already come into a spot of grace and didn't see.

The next shock, six days later, was much worse. It wasn't connected to chemo, except in my mind. It was just one of those awful coincidences, the kind that, inexplicably terrible, can smack you off balance in the best of times.

The first Monday after chemotherapy, I'd left work early. No one around the office seemed to care if I came or went. Since word of my illness had gone around, hardly anyone spoke to me. Walking home in the patchy late-afternoon light, I turned onto Central Park South and saw, coming toward me, an editor I knew, Hope Palmer. "Hope, how are you?" I asked, but I could see she wasn't well. She was jittery, disheveled, an unkempt version of the elegant woman I'd met four years earlier on assignment in Rio. Hope had been there on assignment, too, for the magazine where she worked, a slick monthly about the rich that was always lousy with diamond ads. If she hadn't worked at the place, she would have been a target subscriber. Tousled blonde, slim as a cigarette, she was from an aristocratic California family and breathed good taste. She'd had a glamorous early marriage to a well-known architect, made more glamorous still by its tragic but unspecified ending, and her work now consisted of flying around the world and selecting fine-boned specimens for the monthly's cover. When we'd first met, I'd thought Hope's life was perfectly cast, but then cracks started to show and it was hard to tell what was causing them.

"I have to get out of the magazine," she'd said abruptly during a lunch we'd had two months before. This confidence, and the intensity of it, caught me by surprise. We were merely casual acquaintances.

"I don't know. I don't know. They might be taking away my expense account," she said when I asked her why.

"Where do you think you'd like to go?" I asked, and she named the magazine that had just hired me. "That's the only place I can think of I'd like to work," she added. The lunch left me irritated—I hadn't been expecting to be cruised—but also vaguely concerned. She seemed even more agitated than someone worried for her job should be. At times she'd looked distracted, as if she were hearing a screech of words she couldn't quite make out.

Now, on the street, I found I was repeating our conversation of two months ago.

"I'm bad. I'm really not good," Hope said. Her spare manners had been worn down by something that showed wild in her eyes. "I need to get out of my job."

"Where would you like to go?" I asked before remembering that she'd told me already. She told me again. She wanted to go where I worked.

"I, um, don't think there's anything open right now," I said, hoping my annoyance wasn't visible. I had the oddest sensation, disturbing and fleeting, that she was asking for my life. Since I was now in a position of having to fight for it myself, this exchange struck me as dangerous.

"I have to get uptown," I said. "I'll call you." And as she turned, I thought, She looks haunted.

The encounter had vanished from my mind when, two nights later, the phone rang.

"Did you hear?" a friend said.

"No, what?" I asked.

The day after we'd met up on the edge of Central Park, Hope had left work early, gone home, and killed herself. She'd taken four hundred aspirins ("Do you know how long that would have taken her to do?" my friend said. "Four hundred aspirins is four bottles. She had to have been determined") and then, apparently, changed her mind. Calling her boss, she'd pled, "Help me. I don't want to die," but by the time the ambulance arrived, her heart was giving out.

"You must have felt like, 'Here, if you want to die so much, go ahead and take my cancer,'" a woman who'd had the disease her-

self said when I told her the story. But I hadn't. All suicides provoke guilt and bewilderment, and that's what I felt at first—*if only
I'd said, "Let's go for a coffee," been nicer, tried to help her find work.*
In the phone call informing me, my friend had suggested reasons,
all of which seemed, of course, inadequate. Hope had had a
breakup recently, she told me, with a photographer. Hope had
just gone on antidepressants, and they say that can happen—
sometimes the pills make you feel just better enough that you find
the energy to kill yourself. Each time we spoke her name, we
stammered or gave a nervous laugh, for in the context of the discussion, it sounded like we were making a bad joke.

When the shock had subsided, a detail continued to nag at me.
In the middle of trying to kill herself, she'd called her boss? Had she
really been that obsessed with her work? Suicide's been described
as the "ultimate fuck-you gesture," and perhaps that's what she'd
intended—to show an office that had come to seem monstrous
just how bad they'd made her feel. Or perhaps she'd had no
friends to call. Either way, I thought, what a sorrow, and what a
waste. I considered how she'd been smart and how if she'd held
on, she might have found a way to hoist herself over the rough
patch, or trudge through. I considered, too, how she'd embodied
everything the culture held valuable, and how cheap that irony
was. Fine appearances never saved anyone, but we always think
they will.

Another irony became apparent to me only later, and that was
this: Hope had envied my life, and I'd envied hers, and we'd both
been fooled by surfaces.

The next week, my hair still held but my old existence was thin-
ning out dramatically. Most people still didn't know and I didn't
tell them. I continued to keep up the motions, and the appointments I'd made before. I had tea at the Royalton with a writer
dressed in black, whose hair was short and cropped except for one

long, skinny pigtail down her back. Sade was playing in the background. Her muted sadness intensified my mood. *I met him by the pool at the Chateau Marmont . . .* I tuned in to hear the writer say, and a thought came to me: I'm not like you anymore. In Cancerland, hip is a useless commodity.

I went to see a psychic. I'd booked him some time before, when I was simply a woman going through a divorce. He charged more money than a high-priced shrink and spent as much time boasting about his psychic prowess as he did coughing up the prognostications. Of the many celebrity clients whose names he dropped, not one was still alive and therefore able to contact a lawyer, except, perhaps, through a channeler. One of his mystic revelations was true—I had been involved with a light-haired Gemini, Diego—but the rest were off. My odds of moving to California or into television in the next year were minuscule. By the end of the hour, I was unhappy that I'd come. I didn't think one Gemini was worth $150—I could have told him that going in.

When we got to the questions part, I sat up. "How's my health?" I asked, feigning innocence, aware that, just then, I looked like I was in the pink of it. "Great. Great," he said. "You just need to chew your food more slowly." "Oh yeah?" I pounced. "I have breast cancer." "Well, you weren't supposed to get it," he snapped, in a tone that implied apologies could be in order.

Other than a continuing fetid taste in my mouth, I did feel all right, but then one morning when the alarm went off, I didn't want to get up. My body was just heavy, and the pull of the bed was strong. You're faking it, I chided myself, the old Christian Science influence kicking in, but I allowed myself to phone in sick anyway. With all that's been happening, I thought, it's okay to play hooky once or twice.

"When did you have chemo? Eight or nine days ago?" the oncologist asked when I called, just to be safe. "That's about right."

About right for what? I thought. His laid-back manner, previously a comfort, was, at this moment, irksome. What was he doing, springing something on me, springing a bad surprise?

"This is about the time when you get a dip," he said. "A week or so after chemo, your blood counts fall. Do you feel like you have the flu?"

I hadn't before I called, but now, I realized, maybe I did.

"Don't worry. It'll pass. Take it easy for a few days."

I told him about my hand, how a hard angry pebble had risen up in the veins. It still hurt.

"Yep, we need to get you a catheter," he said casually, as someone might remark, "Fine. Then I'll meet you at nine." Again, he'd clearly been expecting the report and, again, his foreknowledge made me mad. If he'd known all this was inevitable, why had he seemed so relaxed before? It was as if he'd told me a lie. But all he'd done was omit mention of the many potential chemotherapy reactions. That was fine; I didn't want to know every possibility. The trouble was his manner: If he was going to seem placid all the time, how would I be able to read him?

I still hadn't learned that oncologists often appear as laid-back as Buddhist monks. It's a necessary affect, a defense against the pleading and desperation that surrounds them.

Chemotherapy, he explained, had burned out my veins (*in just one round?*), but he'd call Victor and ask him to install a catheter in my chest. "It'll make chemo much easier," he said.

After we spoke, I was surprised to find I was in the grips of a full-fledged chemo side effect, when ten minutes before, I'd only been playing hooky. By ten A.M. I saw that, yes, the condition was flulike indeed. By eleven I described it to friends who called as "It's like I've been flattened by a truck!" By noon I was staggering, Bette Davis–style, the five blocks to the bookstore. On my return, I took the time to slump against a building, for good measure. "It's like I was slogging through oatmeal!" I phoned Michelle to report when I got back. By four I was still bravely bearing up, but by five, after Oprah, I was getting pettish and bored.

By nine the next morning, I was back at my desk. I'd had the experience. I was ready to move on.

My oncologist had other ideas. "Victor thinks he can probably see you tomorrow," he phoned to say. "I'd like to get that catheter in by next week."

In Victor's office I listened nervously as he detailed the procedure. ". . . install a Mediport under your skin just below your collarbone, then run a line up your neck and attach it to your jugular so that . . ." he was explaining. The mention of my jugular vein jerked me away from the blur state I'd been drifting toward. When my niece, Katie, had died the year before, it was because of a botched operation. A surgeon had slipped and sliced her jugular.

Informed breast cancer patients discuss their worries with their doctors, all the books had said, evoking reassuring images of comfortable tête-à-têtes. Those authors hadn't made the acquaintance of my surgeon.

"Oh, yeah, right, I'm really going to sever your jugular," he snorted.

"Oh, yeah, I do it every month," he exclaimed, eyebrows raised and voice cracking.

Perhaps this upsetting inference made him forget the warnings he'd intended to deliver on how uncomfortable the catheter would be at first. At any rate, I was completely unprepared when I woke in the recovery room with what felt, as a friend who's had one described it, like a space station embedded in my chest. On the cab ride home, I tried to hold my head high as a dancer's, unnerved by the tube running up the inside of my neck. Each bump made me groan in pain and worry that the thing might come dislodged. It was a few weeks before I lost the stiff Tin Man pose.

———————

When the fury hit, it hit full force. Objects flew past me in the fractal storm. Remnants of my old life pummeled me into free fall, slamming me off ledges where I'd hunkered down. The growl was a roar was a snarl was a squeal that boxed and sliced me. Shapes shifted in the darkness, but by the end that didn't matter because by then I was nearly blind, I was chemo blind. Aureoles obscured figures and the light was no longer an ocean. It stung me. It made me squint. Months in, I spent hours in bed staring at the patterns of the bricks in the building across the street, unable to read, and I almost didn't care. For one thing, I was listless; for another, I'd had enough.

By the end, I didn't want to look anymore.

The storm smashed down. Its constant roar pulled me into a trance. *This is what happens*, I noted with bemusement when my hair started to fall, first in little bundles of five or ten strands, then in locks, then hunks. *You leave pieces of yourself all over town.* But this is what really happened: The roar was white noise against reality. "I'm just, I'm just so depressed," I told the woman who answered the phone at a cancer hot line. "Do you think that could be because all my hair fell out today?" By the time my hair was gone, I'd retreated into a sere, brambly corner of the harsh new land. By April, without quite avowing it, I was dwelling there almost full time, only occasionally able, with effort, to scramble out and back into the other world. The border divide was receding by the day.

One problem was that the provisions I'd bought marked me as an inhabitant of Cancerland. The wig, the scarves were shibboleths. Once I was forced into putting them on, I could no longer easily pass. The wig was brassy and coarse, too big. I thought I looked like I was balancing a dead animal on my head. I probably didn't, but after a while, I gave it up and wore scarves. By late April, whenever I was able to return, it was as a visitor. Sometimes I still could deceive people. Once, in the reception area of the magazine, as I passed by in a head wrap, a teenage model called, "Oooo! Like your look!" And the apartment's lessor, out of sight in California, hadn't yet learned.

"What if my hair clogs the pipes and she has to get a plumber in?" I'd worried to Michelle, a couple of days before I expected it to fall. "She'd kick me out in a second."

"Why don't you get one of those plastic catchers for the drain," Michelle said, and her suggestion was a good one. Years on, I read an article that gave several useful ideas. A hair net for night would have helped, too.

Michelle called every day. As a friend to someone with cancer, she soared. "How's it going?" she'd ask each morning, with only the lightest concern in her voice. This was a good tone to take; when people sounded frightened, they scared me. She waited to see if I'd mention the illness. If I didn't, neither did she, and through following my lead, she gave me the gift of being able to pretend, when I needed to, that I was having a normal life. On mornings when I wanted to talk, she was intent on listening, careful in her responses. She gently made her presence known in ways that made me aware that I was being watched out for.

Not everyone had her skill. For a while, in fact, it seemed that nobody but Michelle could say the right thing. Some people were well-meaning but thick. A colleague took me out and described, at length, her sister-in-law's death from cancer. "Breast cancer?" she began. "You know, my brother's wife had that." The association seemed to jog her memory but not her brains. Some people were well-meaning but awkward. In the beginning, my father was unable to say the word *cancer*, and his inability drove me wild. For one thing, it spread through the family. "Kathy doesn't like to talk about it," I found out he'd been telling relatives, which explained the wariness I'd heard when they called. "That's not true! He's the one that doesn't want to discuss it," I protested, too angry to see that his stonewalling grew out of deep fear, which in turn was the result of deep love. It wasn't till frustration wore me down that I learned to bask in the sweetness of any good intent and ignore most words that came out wrong.

"How *are* you?" I would hear this refrain ten times in a morning, each time the phone rang. No one realized I'd already delivered the report a half dozen times that day, or that I was at my desk trying to hang on to the semblance of a working life. Sometimes I had to stretch for news. Frequently nothing was happening. Most often, cancer is boring, like a tedious second job that demands extreme amounts of drudge work, time, and patience.

I hated when I got cast as someone's soap opera. If the interest was vicarious, the concern made me recoil. "I'm fine," I'd say, and be exasperated when someone would insist, "No, really. Tell me. How *are* you?"

I was exasperated a lot. Partly I was to blame, being much too judgmental of responses. It took me forever to understand that we were, all of us, winging it. My friends and I were young. We hadn't yet moved into middle age, with its repetitions of illness and loss. We weren't practiced. It wasn't my fault, or theirs, if I was the virgin, the test case. But if I was being made an example of, so they were to me, for we are all of us examples to one another, all the time, during crises and while in the muddle of the commonplace. Looking back, I think that the kind and the cruel (and there were a few of those) were, in one regard, equal. Though in different guises, they appeared as teachers and what they both taught me about was love.

From the kind, I learned about love for others.

From the cruel, I learned, the hard way, about love for myself. In a few stinging instances, I had to decide that if I was ever going to love myself, I would have to be selective in who could come near. Until I became sick, I didn't know that some people really could be cruel to the point of evil.

In between the kind and the cruel, there were the bumblers, and in retrospect, I love them the best. They were there, I think, for respite.

"God speaks through events," the theologian Frederick Buechner writes, and during cancer, I was treated to a few divine comedies. One time the humor was of the black, battlefield variety, the kind that, in cancer support groups, keeps things roiling. "There's someone I want to fix you up with," a woman, a writer and shrink I'd met only once before, said over lunch. She'd called because my new boss had asked her to. She'd had cancer once. He thought she could help.

"No kidding?" I said, my head swelling at this testimony to my charm. Regard—even without hair, I was a magnet for matchmakers.

"Yes, and he's wonderful," she continued. "He's about forty, and good-looking, and really spiritual. Clarence and I taught a death-and-dying workshop together. That's how we met. He's really evolved. He went to theology school."

"Me, too," I said. "I was a religion major."

"And he's got red hair, and he's really cute, and best of all"— she paused—"he's one of us!"

One of us? She can't mean—

"Yes, he is. He has leukemia. Can you believe it? After teaching death and dying, he gets leukemia!"

I was at a loss for words.

"I've told him all about you, but he's a little reluctant." She shook her head, smiling at his silliness. "He said, 'Janie, leave me alone. I've got leukemia. I don't want to go on a date.'"

"Well, you know, if that's how he feels . . ."

"He's worried he might be a burden to you. I just said, 'Clarence, you let *her* be the judge of that.'"

"Oh, no, no. It's probably better if he decides."

"Really, he's doing pretty well. He's just a little florid from the chemo. And he gets winded when he goes up hills," she said. She was giving new meaning to the phrase "You two would have so much in common."

There is no way this is happening, I thought. It was, but the date didn't. Clarence never called. Either he couldn't be prodded or he wasn't up for taking the hills. Or worse—I didn't really want to know how much.

Afterward the whole thing struck me as funny. Cancer humor is like the Zen laugh; it's a way of gathering back forces, a means of breathing in absurdity, darkness, and pain and blowing them out in one great, joyous guffaw. It is, finally, a form of power, laced with machismo. *Fuck you, death. I laugh at you.*

It doesn't always translate across the divide, however, as I discovered when I tried to entertain my father with the story.

"This woman did *what?*" he said, appalled. This was the man who wasn't up yet to saying the word, much less to hearing outtakes from the dating lives of cancer patients, especially not one who was his daughter.

"Yeah, and the guy had, like, leukemia," I repeated, laughing harder. His silence told me he thought I was cracking, not cracking up. Maybe I was. It wouldn't have been the last time cancer made me crazy.

MERCY

THE CHEMOTHERAPY STARTED TO TAKE ME DOWN. THE second time was much harder. The drugs, in the build, were gathering force. I was losing stamina.

The second time, I was a mess.

For one thing, the sublet's owner chose that week to come back to town for a stay, and I had to move out. Pride went before and after the fall of my hair. Neophyte that I was, I didn't want to be treated differently because I was ill, so I continued not to tell her. I thought if I said anything, I would be like Blanche Dubois, trying to depend on the kindness of strangers. But the lessor was not a passing stranger, and Blanche hadn't been sick, and the truth was, I was trying to pretend to one of the few people who didn't know that I was leading the good life.

My ego was tripping me up.

It's easy now to see that I should have called the woman, explained the extenuating circumstances, and asked for a reprieve, but I couldn't. I had my pride, even if that pride was bluster, a cover for the fact that I didn't expect compassionate treatment from anyone—not surprising, since I had so little compassion for myself. I was long on self-pity, and so pity is what I thought I'd receive.

I steamed with indignation, till it clung to me like smoke: *Poor little cancer patient, has to beg for permission just to stay.* Forget it, I wouldn't. I wouldn't ask. Packing a week's worth of clothes, I moved downtown to a friend's. I thought I was proving my strength and independence. Actually I was refusing to fight.

Around this time, a refrain started running through my life. "Be good to yourself," someone would say. "Go easy on yourself," a friend would advise. I'd nod—*Gee, thanks, I will*—but I had no idea what they were talking about. "Be good to yourself"—it sounded like the credo of one of those petulant, harshly made-up women you saw on the jitney to the Hamptons. What were these people telling me to do? Buy things? I had. While married, I'd been frugal, but since the divorce and my conversion to the good life, I'd been indulging a series of whims. I'd bought CDs by the stack, silk blouses I never thought to put on, workout wear I didn't need, an antique Japanese tea container painted with scenes of a moon-viewing party, just because I felt like it. In my divorce haze, I'd seen these purchases as insignias of the life, but now, spotlighted by major illness, they looked like trinkets, pathetic. "Go out and get yourself something nice," a woman who'd heard my bad news said, but I didn't want to, just as I didn't want to continue to work till ten at night anymore. New shoes, job accolades, weren't going to help me improve my health, were ridiculous amulets against mortality. Thinking about it, I was depressed to see I'd been taking my spiritual and mental health cues from ads. I'd been Just Doing It and Being the Best That I Could Be. So, I suspected, had Hope. So was most everyone I knew. But this perception left me at a loss: If the consumer—the achievers' and acquirers'—life wasn't the good life, how the hell were you supposed to be good to yourself?

Well, you could, if you were a cancer patient heading into the second treatment, do precisely the opposite of what I did. First, I didn't ask anyone to be with me. Human contact—what for? I was just going to zip in and out, get the job done. Second, temporarily uprooted from the sublet, I headed straight for the most depressing place I knew: a dingy fourth-floor walkup on a hard-core stretch of Tompkins Square Park that belonged to the friend who'd recently gotten married—probably to get herself out of it, I decided while unpacking. On my one previous overnight stay, the night of the Mystery Date match, I hadn't minded its low-rent qualities: the walls that were grimy, the floors that creaked, the bathtub carpeted with moss. The street din charged me. It beat out a funky bass. But now that chemo was heightening my senses, I noticed that the garbage cans from the macrobiotic restaurant below gave off an unhealthy stench. The street noise wasn't syncopation that night, not a kind of jazz. It was catcalls and bellows of the staggerers and too-hip on their rush of drugs and fight and other hungers in conversion.

Before, I'd been secretly drawn to ugliness. I liked a good neon buzz, a strong visual assault by strip mall. Squalor (in containment, of course) had its appeal. I went in for aesthetic abrasion, for abrasion is protection. It raises calluses. But now, in this sad, stripped-down tenement above Tompkins Square, the Adriamycin was playing shaman with me, sanding through roughness and carapace to skin, uncovering senses that had been dulled by years of work and drink and love imploded.

It was also, five hours after the injection, producing an intense, itchy flush. The cool night air of April flamed my forehead, made me shiver. Bonner had sworn that afternoon that he'd skipped the knockout drugs, but by nine o'clock, whatever cocktail he'd mixed was putting me out. Outside, on the street, the baseline was just building, however. Tires squealed, a buddy roared to a friend, the restaurant's clatter rose and broke, rose and broke. By ten I was desperate with exhaustion. By two I finally fell asleep, but not before, in just a few hours of auditory immersion, I'd got my fill of ugliness for life.

Two hours later, at four A.M., my eyes opened in pain and surprise, but for a minute, I couldn't come fully awake. Goddamn health food, I thought, groggily blaming the fermenting soybean odor for the deep, blasting nausea that had fired me out of sleep. Then I remembered. This wasn't soy. Panicked, I struggled to untangle the blankets from my legs before the water in my mouth swelled to waves. The bathroom was a long skid down a distant dark hallway, but I made it.

I spent eight hours, off and on, in the bathroom that day. Around six, scared and sweaty, I phoned Diego. He was there in fifteen minutes and stayed till ten, then left during a calm that made us think the vomiting had stopped. It hadn't. At ten-thirty, hoarse, I called Diego again.

"Did you try the Compazine?" Bonner asked when he phoned me back at noon. "It works great. I use it myself on ski trips when I'm hungover. Didn't I give you a prescription?" He had, but I'd forgotten. My familiarity with drugs was limited to the illegal ones from my teenage years. I'd stuffed the prescription somewhere. Diego and I tore up my bags and suitcase until we found it. Within a half hour, my stomach was quiet, although my legs were still rubber when I went to Michelle's for dinner that night. "I threw up for eight hours straight, then showed up at a dinner party," I used to boast, till I met a few too many breast cancer vets who sounded like they were telling the story of how they'd massively ambushed the gooks.

From the first, Diego put himself on call for me. Initially I was hesitant to turn to him. It didn't seem right. I'd been the one to walk out. ("And you left me for nobody," he'd pointed out. "I could see if you had left me for a blond, eighteen-year-old surfer, but you didn't. You left me for no one.") But from the minute I told him the news, he made it clear that he'd set his anger aside and be available however I needed him.

In the strange, twilight world of the illness, Diego was changed up too. The Adriamycin was flowing through me, but it worked as shaman to him as well. It made him a nurturer. Now that compassion and goodwill weren't demanded by a marriage contract but by a higher purpose, he was able to give freely. Arriving in the evening, he'd lie with me in the dim light, stroking my hand while I stared at the TV. His voice was succor, a low, lilting croon. "Are you okay? Do you think you need to sleep now?" He needed to prove that he was not a bad guy, that he had loved me and that he loved me still. He proved it again and again, till I winced at the guilt he so obviously bore.

I forgave him, and in the forgiving I saw that my martyr pose had been a sham. Married, I'd shouted, "You make me sick." But in these extreme conditions, I couldn't go the next step and hold him accountable for giving me cancer. That would be outrageous. In parodying my complaint, the illness made me admit that Diego wasn't the afflictor and I wasn't the afflicted. We'd been playing at those roles and the game had gone too far. I wasn't the role anymore. I wasn't a victim.

When I comprehended that, I could begin the fight.

Looking back, I can't believe that either of us was able to navigate the long, land-mined stretch of that spring and summer. Just prior to the diagnosis, we were furious with each other. We were, neither of us, overly mature. But we'd been relying on our stereotypes for so long, it was a relief to shuck them, to stop having to be a hot-tempered Argentine and a thin-blooded WASP and rejoin as two human beings, one who'd vowed to do the right thing and help keep the other alive. We'd been locked into clangorous marital battles for so long, it was good to be forced to give them up.

The situation knocked sense into us. It slapped us silly. Cancer elicited the kind of spurring insight that ten years of marriage counseling never would have. *Life is short*, it cackled. *You two better figure out how you're going to get along.*

It wasn't easy. We rose to the challenge, but sometimes we came up duking it out.

Once I made the mistake of trying to rekindle passion. Two months into chemo, I was avoiding mirrors. I loathed seeing the worm woman, hairless and white, who always glanced away. Diego and I were spending a lot of time together on our backs. I wanted reassurance, and one night I reached over. For the first time ever, we failed in bed, and hurt, I lashed out. "Forget it," I said. "Don't bother. I don't want a mercy fuck." "Well, that's exactly what this was," he replied. We fought, then he jammed on his clothes and left. As soon as the door closed, I cried till I choked. I was disgusting—just look!—not a woman, a thing. Self-pity welled up, blocking all understanding of how I'd just set us both up. It made it easy to despise him, to despise the fact that I'd automatically won the round—for no matter how spiteful I'd been, he'd been mean to a cancer patient. The feeling, I'm sure, was mutual. But that night he called to see if I needed anything.

My marriage was a series of lessons in destruction; its dissolution taught me about love. By joining together, we were able to disentangle and move on. Illness healed our rift. For a time I couldn't turn around without hitting up against a paradox.

It's miscalculated paradox that makes some patients proclaim, "Cancer was the best thing that ever happened to me!" Cancer is not the best anything, except, in too many instances, killer. It's savage and cruel; it can cripple people, maim them, leave them begging for air, or hope, or death. Cancer was one of the worst things that ever happened to me, but in that fact exists the most enduring of its paradoxes: My friendship with Diego, which came out of it, is one of the best.

By May I was in the eye of the storm. A silence settled on me, but it wasn't a comfort, it was a warning. The light was yellow all day, not just toward evening. The low light blurred my vision, so at first I didn't see that a ghost had begun to dog me. It followed me everywhere. At night it stood outside the bedroom door and wailed till I was forced to get up and try to comfort it. At any time during the day, it would put its hands over my eyes and croak into my ear, "You're all alone. There's no one left." One time when I was trying to have a business lunch at the Oyster Bar, it stood behind my chair and hissed, "You don't deserve to eat," until I couldn't even swallow. The ghost would not stay where it belonged, in Cancerland. When I slipped out, it did, too.

The ghost gave voice to the disease. With its intensifying properties, cancer stirs up your basest neuroses. It magnifies your oldest fears. Thought you'd gotten over the hurt of those playground slights from third grade? Guess what: It's back and you're bald. Cancer will show you exactly where you've got your psychic work cut out for you.

On the job, I wasn't being chosen for teams, or projects, or much of anything. In *Bang the Drum Slowly*, it had escaped my notice that the baseball team had wanted to trade Robert De Niro as soon as they learned he had Hodgkin's. I should have paid closer attention.

"I thought I was going to be working with you," the new writer said, appearing unexpectedly in my office one morning to explain that the editor had called and asked him to come in. "I agreed to do the piece, and then he asked Julia Anderson to come to his office. He said she would be working with me. I thought it was going to be you. Hey, how come you're wearing that hat?" he added, not improving my mood.

Right after I'd started working there, I'd wooed the writer with lunches and calls, arguing that he should try us on a piece, it could be fun. A month later, he won a National Magazine Award, and a month after that, I was pleased when he said he thought he'd have time. I reported his availability to my boss. The writer and I hadn't spoken since. Apparently the deal had been closed.

"Why did you do that? Why did you give him to Julia?" I asked when I got the editor on the phone. "I brought him in."

"Look. Julia has paid her dues. You haven't," he said. He'd hung up before I could ask: And how can I pay them if you won't let me work?

The man had hired employees before and they'd lost their heads. Now he'd hired one who'd lost her hair, and he didn't know what to do.

Nor did I. In hindsight, I think, the best move I could have made would have been to hole up in my apartment and out of view until chemotherapy was over. But I hated staying home, where there was no one to talk to and nothing to do but think. Not that the office provided multiple distractions. The couple of responsibilities I had, editing a column of essays by women writers, assigning the travel pieces, didn't take long. I was raring to prove myself on larger features, but since March, I couldn't get a feature idea or writer approved to save my life. Which, in a way, is what I was after.

Before, in all those long, slogging days I'd put in at a desk, I'd never bothered (never had time, I would have said) to develop outside interests. My work had been my passion, my social life, my entertainment, the focus of my thought and conversation, the common bond in my marriage. "We had nothing to talk about," I'd tell my friends, all in the business, after a date with a man who wasn't.

My work was me. For the first decade of my adult life, when I'd mainly done well, this had been a fine substitution for self. Now, no matter how hard I tried, I was bombing. With each still-born effort, with each proposal that never received a reply, with each clumsy attempt I made to join the others in the editor's office for drinks (silence when I entered, then the conversation would haltingly resume, but no one would engage me and I'd stand alone grinning stupidly and calculating how long before I could leave), with each accumulating failure, I sunk down further, became more afraid that I wasn't just suffering losses from cancer, but that I was becoming one big net loss, a loser.

Be careful of what you petition the gods, I reminded myself one day when another story idea was shot down. I'd wanted to be cured of workaholism. I just hadn't expected to be flung into rehab and back onto myself.

My case wasn't helped by the fact that the editor's mother had cancer. "She doesn't know how sick she is," he'd said, darkly, during one of the few talks we'd had since I'd begun coming to work in scarves. I worried I was a reminder. I was pretty sure I was.

Sometimes I seemed to be in a hallucinatory flashback from the playground. I'd look up and see the editor gathering the other senior staff members for lunch and realize I wasn't being included. Days would go by and no one would speak to me. One morning an assistant I didn't know well appeared at my door. "I just want to tell you," she said shyly, "that I think you're brave." I stared at her dumbly. This was the first person who'd spoken to me in the office in two weeks. I nodded. I couldn't answer. If I had, I'd have started to cry.

It took years for me to understand that the situation was awkward. My coworkers didn't know what to say. But in their distance, I thought I was being shunned. A loneliness settled in that was so deep, it terrified me. (With good reason, I later learned, when I came upon studies showing that cancer patients who don't have social support tend to die sooner. Or some of them do. One study conducted in Scandinavia indicated that while the lack of a social network was "a risk" for women with cancer, the *existence* of one, on the other hand, was actually a risk for men. Jeesh, I thought—maybe all those guys who hate to socialize aren't kidding.)

Loneliness is one of cancer's sly, nasty tricks. It's built into the disease in a way that's not true with, say, heart trouble. The books had warned I'd feel it. They hadn't suggested how profound it would be.

Once the loneliness took hold, I couldn't shake it. It stopped being circumstantial and became constant. The books blamed isolation, but in reality it infiltrated my body. I could have been with twenty friends, had one eternal lover, and it still would have plagued me.

The loneliness that comes with cancer is virulent, malignant, a reflection of the disease. In one sense, it is the disease, or at least an aspect of it. When the heart fails, for instance, it goes out like a faithful old hound, beating feebly right up to the end, trying to do its best. Cancer, however, is a panther, voracious but willing to bide its time. The heart stays put. It doesn't creep through the body, a silent stalker, slashing out with no more than the rustle of a warning to feast on its prey: your organs. You.

And yet the cancer, too, is you. It's not, as far as we know, brought on by an airborne microbe. It's not a foreign agent, not the flu; you don't catch it. It's a cellular part of you turned wild, ungovernable. It is you divided against yourself. It is your body made sinister, made into its own assailant—its own assassin, if medical treatment or stasis fails.

If your body is divided within, how can you not feel divided from the world? If you can no longer trust yourself at your core, how can you trust anyone else? It's these properties of cancer that cause the loneliness, not the tendency for some people to shy away.

Cancer lies. It tells you there are other reasons why you feel so despondent. And since it likes to piggyback onto other misfortunes, usually there are. "First my lover broke up with me," a woman I met in a support group said. "Then my mother was hit by a truck and killed. I lost my job and I was diagnosed. All in one year. I'm just so fucking lonely," she sighed.

Misfortune can exaggerate the unhappiness a patient feels, but I don't think it creates it. Loneliness is intrinsic to cancer, I believe in more paranoid moments, because loneliness is one of its killing tools. It's useful. Malignant tumors swell till they cut off nourishment. Malignant despair grows till it weakens and starves the soul. I've seen it happen. After a while some people no longer care.

There are ways to relieve the loneliness. But I was still trying to find them.

"I'm so depressed," I told the Freudian during a phone session one afternoon. I wasn't coming into her office much now, although we'd been careful not to discuss the reason why. The woman would have been delighted to talk anal sex or sibling death wishes till my insurance ran out. But she had no intention of going anywhere near the Big C.

I did, though. I was beginning to be a fighter. I wanted to face cancer square on. Emboldened by distance, I tried.

"This is bad," I said. "Chemo is making me sick all the time. My eyelashes are gone. Dirt gets in my eyes. I'm fed up with not having hair. All I do is lie around. No wonder I'm depressed."

"Believe it or not," the Freudian replied, "all this has to do with your childhood." I was citing biochemical causes, not buried conflict. This was not right.

"Oh, Jesus," I said. "Do you mean to tell me it's not valid for me to feel depressed because I'm on chemotherapy? That it's not legitimate for me to be upset because I'm bald and have cancer? Is that what you're saying? Oh, come on!"

"No, no," she backtracked. "No, you can feel those things."

There was a silence. I relaxed.

"But believe it or not," she said, digging in, "your childhood really does have something to do with how you're feeling." There was no doubt about it: We were going *Totem and Taboo* all the way. She could handle a decent neurotic, the kind who was conflicted between the desire to go away for the summer and the wish to stay in town. ("Wainscot? I had a dream last night in which everyone was calling it 'Waste Not.' Do you think this means I shouldn't rent the house?") She could have even taken on the Wolf Man. But Freud had said nothing about a Worm Woman. And neither, it was clear, would she.

I didn't get rid of her right away. I couldn't stand another ending then. But a while later, a friend, a writer named Ben, asked what my shrink had to say about my cancer.

"Actually, we've never discussed it," I said.

"What?" he said. "You've never discussed your cancer? Fire your shrink."

That was all I needed to hear. The next morning, I picked up the phone, and I did.

NOD

BY JUNE THE DESOLATION WASN'T DEEPENING SO MUCH AS ripening. It was like a sweetish bad odor that hadn't turned all the way. A full whiff made you slightly ill, but you got used to it. After a while, the only way you'd notice it is if you left the room. I wasn't going out much then.

Desolation was becoming consolation. I'd gotten in the habit of repeating to myself all the bad things that had happened. I had to say them because I couldn't believe them, but through repetition they became familiar, and the familiarity itself became an odd sort of comfort. Alone at night, I told them to the ghost. "I've lost everything," I'd rail. "My marriage! My hair! My stepchildren! My health! My home!" It grinned and nodded. It knew.

Talk like this was a mistake outside the house. It drew the gawkers. But I wasn't sure how to refer to my inner life. "I'm so upset about Gilda Radner," I began one lunch with two friends. In the middle of reading the comedienne's book, an account of her struggle with ovarian cancer, I heard on the radio that she'd died. I'd learned the news that morning and I was in shock. It was on my mind as I sat down, so I mentioned it, but as soon as I did, I wished I hadn't. My friends looked uncomfortable. They fumbled for something to say. I hadn't meant to call attention to my own situation, but suddenly I saw that of course that's what I'd done. *A cancer patient saddened by the death of another cancer patient:*

Wasn't that what I was? Embarrassment silenced me for the rest of the lunch.

I was trying to treat cancer as if it were just another part of my life, but that was impossible. If I referred to it, even casually, I gave any conversation immediate existential overtones. But if I didn't talk about it, I felt lonely, set apart. I wasn't sure how to strike a balance.

"People don't want to hear about it," a great-aunt who'd had cancer said. It was the assumption of her generation. This idea surprised me. I'd been operating on generational assumptions of my own. Like everyone my age, I'd been raised to get things off my chest. Therapy had instilled in us a conviction in the power of confession. We reveled in a carefully proscribed form of candor, the honesty of talk shows (self-revelations about sex or degradation, for instance, but never venality or arrogance or the other, more banal sins that actually made us look bad). People my age told all. In the first, terrible rush of the illness, so did I. Cancer was never far from my mind—what else was I going to discuss? But I quickly found that my great-aunt had a point. Some people didn't want to hear about it. And some people did but for the wrong reasons. And some, like my father, wanted to but weren't easily able. They were afraid. (The Freudian was in a different category. She'd been paid to listen and wouldn't, which constitutes not doing her job.) After a few uneasy receptions, I began to temper myself, to choose the moment and the ear more carefully, and in the process, I learned about dignity.

These were tough lessons. Without knowing it, I'd stumbled into another one of cancer's traps: By demanding constant vigilance, it makes you self-absorbed. This enforced narcissism, in turn, contributes to distancing you from everyone around you. Cancer is infantile in its demands; it never gives you a rest. It feints, it whispers. "Here, I'm over here," it calls, and you look, but it isn't. That was just a headache, not the next pyrotechnic, not the seedling of a tumor in your brain.

Monitor your own body long enough, and if you have an ongoing relationship with an oncologist, you are guaranteed to come down with what my meditation teacher calls "fingernail cancer." The pain was nothing, but you phoned it in and you feel silly for having reported it. Doubt sets in, and any ghosts in your house will jabber and hoot, and the next time you might not call, which makes it worse. You'll just stay on watch, and worry.

What are you watching? Yourself. You're spending hours, days, regarding yourself, and not other people, not the world. You're distracted at dinner with a friend, lose the thread at movies. A gulf is widening between you and others. As the disease and its drama absorb you, it can get harder to find a way to bridge the chasm, to get back.

A few months into chemotherapy, I perceived that I had to find ways to stay connected to the world. The hum of cancer's self-absorption started to make me nervous. The disease was becoming a siren, and its call—my hair! my house!—was pulling me out to a precipice in the land that, I recognized now, existed between life and death. Sometimes, close to the sharp edge of a shelf, I'd turn and skitter back. When I'd tried to look over, I couldn't see down.

I forced myself to reconsider the verses: My marriage!—but it had always been precarious, a gamble. My hair!—this one was harder; I'd stopped believing it would come back. My stepchildren!—I missed them, but in fact, there'd been a dim pane between us all along. My home!—I was only between apartments, not homeless. It was time I started to look.

I had to learn to avoid the dark angels who pumped up the volume. *It's just so awful, you must feel terrible.* These were the acquaintances who wouldn't take "I'm okay" for an answer. They came in the guise of Florence Nightingale, but they weren't healers; they left me feeling shaky, as if I were an incarnation of illness, of absolute despair. *You must just feel totally devastated, first your marriage and now . . . this. And you were so happy in that other job, too. It's such a shame you switched when you did.* They were attracted to my misery in an attempt to escape their own.

I devised a new rule: Only associate with people whose obsession with your illness is less than your own. The tip-off was if they acted like you were a person who was only temporarily without hair. I had four or five friends I saw regularly. Sara, for instance, would ask me to join her at an exercise class that was famous for its boot camp techniques. I wasn't about to step foot in the place, but I was thrilled to be asked. Carol got tickets for the theater, Judy included me in invitations to dinner parties I never attended. But the invitations were enough.

Leah treated me bald, and it was all right. She was in a separate category. She had problems different from mine, but equally grave—she'd gotten hit by a car while biking in France—which made her a refreshing companion. We called ourselves the Halt and the Lame Club. The club's main activity was going home early. Leah would invite me to her apartment for pizza and we'd call it a night before the video. Or we'd plan an excursion to the movies and leave after the first shoot-out. "The motto of our club is 'You wanna go?'" we decided.

Nobody, however, equaled Kay, my eighty-three-year-old great-aunt. Kay had been a magazine editor in the 1950s, and she continued to dress all in black. She'd practiced toughness, élan, for so long, she was fluent. "Between my first and my second marriages, I got pregnant," she said over lunch in a pub full of men. "I didn't know who the father was, so I charged them all fifty bucks for the abortion." Heads whipped around. I looked to see if she'd noticed. She was taking a bite of her burger.

On Sundays Kay held a salon of sorts in her long apartment, on Eighty-second and York. Though the Halt and the Lame Club had it over Kay's in terms of pacing, I loved the company there, which was quirky and lively. One of Kay's daughters was a lesbian motorcyclist who taught electronics in prison. The other had had an early, necessary marriage to an infamous writer's gay son. After her son was born, she married again, to a heroin addict, and again, with success, to a musician, and now she was leading a respectable life as an urban archaeologist. That son, now in his twenties, was as talented as he was good-looking, which was considerable. He was a rising bad-boy in the art world, but he didn't have anything on his grandmother.

"I was astounded. Those nurses wouldn't come," Kay said, leaning back in her chair. The week before, she'd been hospitalized, first time ever, for a stomach problem.

"I rang and I rang, but they wouldn't answer." So she'd picked up the phone, dialed 911, and yelled, "Help! I'm sick and I need help!" The man on the other end asked for her name. He asked where she was. "Lenox Hill Hospital, and I can't get a nurse," she'd shouted, banging down the phone. The nurses began looking in more after that.

I loved Kay's stories. My mother, however, was of a different mind. "Oh, really? You've been visiting that woman?" my mother said coolly. "You know she dragged the family name through the mud." While in her thirties, a divorcée, Kay had married my great-uncle, whose main attributes were a certain easy charm and a listing in the *Social Register*. His moral conduct, however, was not rigorous. He drank a lot and he ran around. Two children into it, Kay had had enough. She got in touch with a sharp-witted young lawyer. "I can't pay you," she said when she asked him to take her divorce. "But I can promise the papers will mention your name." Beauty and Society Scoundrel in Bust-Up—she was right; the papers did.

"He tried to flee to the islands," my mother said, indignant at his plight. "But she had him thrown into alimony prison, and he *died* there." I had my doubts about the alimony prison part—my mother was a known embellisher. Nonetheless, rather than having the desired cautionary effect, the story left me deeply impressed with Kay. Here was someone who had the kind of survival skills I needed. I began spending more time with her.

That summer on chemo, I developed a fascination with old age. I read about it, inquired about it, watched what films there were about it—hedges, no doubt, in case I didn't get to live it. Kay indulged me. I'd drill her on what it was like in the sixth and seventh and eighth decade; did it keep getting better? It did, she said. "You rediscover things you've forgotten you liked," she said. "Gangster movies. Or books you loved." I made a note to increase my passions now so I'd have a store to return to later, in the event that I needed one.

Along with Kay's, several friendships took root, and a couple of others strengthened in that nuclear summer. But a few of the weaker ones foundered. I was being reconfigured right down to my atoms, so it would only follow that my relationships would be rearranged, too. At the time, I was distressed. My friendships were like the table of elements, absolute and constant. But two didn't last out the year.

The first ended quickly, when the friend reneged on an offer to stay with me after chemo. "Honey," she phoned to say, just as I was coming in the door from treatment, "the subways have been making me claustrophobic lately. Can't you meet me halfway?"

Metallic water was collecting in my mouth. "I can't," I said, then forgot to call back for so long, it became impossible to call again.

The second wound down over months. It had more to recommend it. This friend could be bright and expansive—she was the one who lent me the Tompkins Square place when I'd been dislodged—but she could also be unexpectedly harsh. "God, first my friend Tina dies of a cocaine overdose, and now you," she said when she found out about the cancer. She was lamenting the rough month she'd had. I was still learning the lesson that whenever you find yourself thinking, They can't mean that, unfortunately, they probably do.

"This disease gave me more compassion for people with real problems," a woman with cancer told me when I first got ill. "But

I have no tolerance anymore for people who whine about nothing." My patience for inflated complaining gave out by the second chemo. My friend's indulgence increased. "Jason and I are hugely upset," she'd called to announce, and I'd brace myself, thinking, What?

"Our humidifier is consuming *a gallon* of water a night," she said. "I am not kidding. An *entire gallon*. Do you know what that means? That means I have to climb all the way up into the loft to change it."

Before long, I'd backed off, but I wasn't sure how to back out until we went to the movies one lunchtime, a month after I'd had radiation. The choice of films had taken elaborate discussion. No matter which I put on the table, she'd countered with the name of an imported Japanese movie I hadn't heard of. After five rounds it became clear there was no other she'd consider, so I agreed.

Ten minutes into the show, I was ready to bolt. Up on the screen, women were wailing as their hair slid out in chunks. Children were bent over, vomiting into the street. The film, it turned out, was a graphic documentary about the effects of radiation poisoning on a Japanese town. I couldn't bear it, and when I glanced over and noticed she was turned toward me, clinically watching my reaction, I saw in an instant: I didn't have to. I got up and left the theater. From then on, I was more careful in making friends.

By June I'd made it past the midpoint, but no one marked the occasion and I didn't notice. I wasn't noticing much of anything by then. Chemo had gone on so long, it had become perpetual: the future, the world without end. My hopelessness was profound. It was quicksand. I was sunk down in it, caught and preserved by despair.

I would lie in bed and grief would flood me and I couldn't distinguish its source: the divorce or the disease. (Forever after, the two would be linked in my mind. When you got divorced, you lost your hair.) Mourning flowed through me on two currents, till sorrow nearly drowned me from within. The sorrow carried me to a conclusion: I had lost too much. In its eddies, I reached a decision. If so much could be taken away, I would not allow myself to want anything again.

I forced myself to stop caring, about anything. I stayed like that for a very long time.

With desire gone, I became like a beast. I moved forward on instinct alone, impeded by the fact that chemotherapy had scrambled my psyche. Used in another context, on prisoners, say, chemo might be regarded as torture, not therapy. But the psyche is primal. It doesn't understand context. It's not able to register that the body is being poisoned to be healed, not punished. The psyche gets pushed too far.

Reality became slippery, and once or twice I lost my grip. At a lunch, I became sure that the reason the other diners had hair and I didn't was that they knew how to grow it. I used to, but I'd forgotten the technique. No, that wasn't right—I wasn't trying hard enough. I was lazy or just dim. Losing the train of conversation, I concentrated on willing my follicles to bloom. I willed them so hard, my head hurt. All day I remained seized by the conviction that baldness was my fault. When the delusion gave and my head cleared, I was ashamed by how mad I'd become.

I confided this episode to a few friends. They tried to console me. "I was just reading about how medicine has come up with technologies that go too far, that overwhelm the patient. Like MRIs that make you claustrophobic. No one stops to ask if the patient can handle them," Michelle said.

"That reminds me of something I heard a concentration camp survivor say," Judy told me. "After a while the women in the camps became convinced that what was happening to them was a natural disaster, like a tornado. It's the only way they could comprehend what was going on."

My friends tried hard, but my illness was a gulf between us. They hadn't been through anything like this. Only once during that summer did I find a bridge. I got a call from a woman named Isabelle. I didn't know her well, but I admired her work. She'd heard I was in a bad way. She wanted to take me to lunch.

When we sat down, she asked how it was going. She leaned forward as she spoke. She sounded genuinely concerned. I wanted to tell her, but I couldn't. This was in the time of my nadir, when misery had left me sledgehammered and dumb. When I didn't answer, she offered an account of her own bad-luck derby, which was a beaut. Not long before, in her thirties, her husband had left her, an arsonist had torched her weekend house, and a cab crash had knocked out her teeth and broken her jaw. I listened intently, intrigued by the fact that it was impossible to square the story with the woman who'd sat down at the table. That woman ran her own magazine. She'd remarried—happily, she said. I didn't doubt that she had. She looked radiant. The story simply didn't match the woman.

"But you're fine," I said cautiously. "But you seem fine."

"I am." She smiled. "I am fine." They were only three words, but they turned me around. In that moment, I made a connection: I could be fine, too. In the blackness that was clouding my soul, I felt something spark. I wasn't so far gone I didn't know what it was: hope. This hope was minuscule—smaller, maybe, than my tumor had first been, a few tinselly molecules, no more—but in the days that followed I held on to it, and it turned out it was big enough to keep me alive.

Had I been more diligent about attending support groups, I might have discovered other bridges out of that darkness. But I could never find a group to stay with. I'd try one for a while, get spooked, drop out. The first I attended, for instance, at a non-profit breast cancer center, was more upsetting than enlightening. "My husband refuses to look at my scar," a woman told the gathering. "He says, 'Why should I? You're just going to die anyway.'" People shifted nervously in their seats. Was this what their husbands were thinking? Was this what would happen to them? The great catalytic support-group effect eluded me. I left in worse spirits than I came.

Bonner made attempts to lighten my mood. He hadn't trained in cancer psych, but he tried. Our best and safest common ground was humor. We gave it feeble tries. "Hey, don't you have to give me marijuana?" I'd inquire. "I thought you were required to by law."

"Go ahead and bring your own down here and smoke it if you want," he said, shrugging. I was tempted by the novelty, though not the reality. The last thing I wanted was to smoke something that lowers your immune system and makes you fat and paranoid. I was already getting those benefits from cancer. But I was amused by the fact that I could legally ingest cannabis, and that my company plan would cover it. "This is the perfect disease for drug-addict transvestites," I told Bonner. "Insurance has to pay for your wig and your pot."

If my jokes were beat, Bonner's bombed. "Don't worry. The hair grows back in eighty-five percent of all cases," he said one day when I was moaning about the loss of mine.

"What?" I cried. "*Eighty-five* percent?"

"I was just kidding." He laughed. I didn't.

I hated the treatments, but I liked seeing him. We had a companionable accord. After chemo he'd motion me into his office and offer me a chair. I'd hang out for a while and he'd confide that his new, second wife was trying to get pregnant, or that he was secretly thinking of moving to Pittsburgh, but don't tell the staff. We'd discuss Diego—I wondered: Should we try again? No, he said, twisting a locking metal puzzle a drug company had sent him. "It's important not to confuse the desire to help with the ability to make it work." He didn't just talk to me about cancer. He acted like I was somebody who had another, real life.

Our conversations on that score were generally short. There wasn't a lot to discuss. But at the end of June, I had a bulletin. "Really? A new apartment?" Bonner said. New, and contractually mine. In what was certainly the fastest real-estate transaction in the history of New York City, I'd bought a place. One afternoon at work, I'd received a call. The lessor's brother had gotten engaged. Her future sister-in-law wanted the sublet. I had a month to get out.

A friend's friend knew about a one-bedroom for sale. I shot down by subway and looked it over. It had floors that buckled where tenants had left the windows open during rains. But it also had original hand-painted Victorian tiles in the bathroom and seven windows, three of them bay, lots of light. I had limited energy. I called the owner and said I'd take it. That night I dreamed the place was missing a bathroom. Having sped through the apartment, I hoped this was just symbolic (parts of me missing? wish fulfillment—I never wanted to spend extended amounts of time in a bathroom again?) and not buried memory.

By the time the lessor called to say the engagement was off and ask me to stay, I was already about to close.

At the signing, I forced my face blank to disguise the fact that a seventh-grade science project was taking place in my stomach. A week later, two friends arrived at the sublet to help me cart out the eleven boxes I'd packed up the summer before. In the move, I lost a gold bracelet and a walking stick a high-school boyfriend had carved me. "It's only stuff," I told my mother, nearly meaning it.

My first night in the apartment, I was upset to discover I'd bought a place that smelled. The kitchen had a brown stench like garbage. The odor was stubborn. No matter how or where I scrubbed, it stayed strong. When it disappeared a few weeks after the end of chemo, I saw that the trouble hadn't been with the apartment, but with my remixed blood chemistry.

I was too weak to buy furniture, and so the place stayed bare through the summer and for a couple of months after that. Bookshelves made up one wall of the living room. They were fine for underwear and shirts. Michelle donated two black director chairs that looked spindly in the front room alone. Diego carried over an old twin mattress, and that's how I rode out the last month of chemo, by a window on the bedroom floor.

The last month of chemo is recorded in my date book—not recorded, to be precise. The earlier pages, spring, are scribbled up black, but by late-May, whole sheaves are mostly unmarked. Now and then, a lunch appears. June 8: "Lucy—Oyster Bar." My sister had come up with her new fiancé, Phil. We'd gone across the street. Over pan roast, they'd asked me to be in their wedding at Labor Day and I'd said yes. Bonner had promised I'd have hair by then.

Otherwise, the days are nearly white, maybe one entry a week. There's a note about a press conference and one about a movie screening, although I don't now recall ever having seen the film. It's possible I sat through it in a chemo fog or, more likely, that I canceled at the last minute, probably without having to offer a reason. People would always exclaim, "Oh, fine! No problem!," before I could get to the explanation.

And on one page, in early July, I've written the name of an eye doctor. I'd been having trouble seeing, I told Bonner and he'd set up an appointment. My eyes were red. Full light hurt them. I pulled back when the ophthalmologist bore down with his beam.

"It's all right," he said afterward. "I didn't find anything. I'll call Bonner and tell him."

"All right?" I repeated. I couldn't see.

"You're fine. Don't worry," he said. "There's no cancer." Cancer? That's what Bonner thought I had—cancer of the eye? His

Zen affect had thrown me again. I felt betrayed again—he'd been so casual in making the appointment ("and you can just stop by when you have a chance"), it hadn't occurred to me he was worried about spread to the eyes. At that moment I understood that from then on, any bodily misfire, no matter how slight, would produce a full-scale medical alert. Cancer is reverse hypochondria. "How are you feeling?" the oncologist asks each visit. "How's your vision? Is it blurry? Have you lost weight? How's your energy? Are you tired? Do you feel any pain, anywhere?" The oncologist runs through every ordinary symptom of the human condition and you learn the hard way that one "yes" will land you in some bulky, groaning machine faster than you can say, "But really, it's not that bad."

I had conjunctivitis, the result of a lowered immune system. And I had fingernails that were peeling off and feet that were raw on the soles where the skin had dropped off in sheets. In the mornings I didn't want to brush my teeth. The toothbrush made my gums bleed. The bristles came out red. By the last chemo, I wasn't a white worm anymore. My thighs and arms were mottled brown and my chest had a black ring of bruise that circled the catheter. I kept dressed all the time so I wouldn't have to look. My eyes stayed bad, I couldn't read. The television had no images just blurs and the voices were muffled by a thick low sound, a roar. "Did you hear that?" I called from the bed, but I was alone. The ghost had stayed for one last watch where it glared fire at me; then it was gone. This time the growl was rapture; I tried not to listen. In the high-rise across the street, dark bricks made a slipstream ripple and I concentrated on that instead. I didn't want to get up. The mattress was flat, but it had power and appetite, it could devour me. It had the power to hold me down. By the end, I couldn't move. I was too sick after a while, and that's what happened.

By the end, I just got too sick.

LINE

IN THE YEAR AFTER CHEMOTHERAPY, I TRIED TO FIND A WAY to lose the bed.

A friend, a practicing Catholic, described a time in her life when she was wretched with guilt over something she'd done. She wouldn't say what her sin was, only that its commission had skewered her sense of self. In her own eyes, she was no longer good. She needed relief.

On vacation in Italy, in a mountain town, she met an old priest and, hoping to put the deed behind her, she confessed, expecting absolution. Instead, he gave her an argument. She couldn't just wipe the action from the record, the priest said. For one thing, that was impossible. For another, it would cost, perhaps even hobble, her. When Jesus healed the paralyzed man after forgiving him his sins, didn't he instruct him to lift up his bed and go home? "He didn't say, Leave the bed. He said, Pick it up, take it with you," the priest argued, advising her to do the same. Without acceptance of our botches, he counseled, we were stuck. We couldn't continue on. We needed their memories as markers: of where we'd been, where we should head, with luck, of how much we'd changed. If we lost or erased them, we'd be without compasses.

After illness, as after sin, the temptation is strong: to flee the bed. "Once treatment ends," an oncologist told me, "people try to isolate the disease, to make it into an episode, into something that just happened. They think that's the best way to defend themselves. They think they can put the cancer into an aluminum box and store it in a far corner of the room, and it's painful to watch them try. They say, 'Now I can get on with my life,' and I want to answer, 'You can't. This *is* your life.'"

By then I'd gone enough rounds with cancer that I didn't shudder when she said this. I agreed. She continued. "I try to tell them, 'You've had all this awful stuff happen to you. Don't just throw it away.' But that's what they do. They try to dive right back into their old life."

In the years immediately after chemo, I kept trying to dive back in, but my old life wouldn't have me. Maybe the trouble was that my earlier life had evaporated, and I was too dazed to notice I was aiming for rock. Or maybe my budding survival instincts were trying to steer me away from the old waters but weren't strong enough yet to propel me full-force into the new. Whatever the case, I kept getting banged and scraped.

Not two weeks after chemo ended, I met a man. I was at a party, still in head wraps; I could feel his interest from across the room. The next day, the host called to say his friend wanted my number. "Okay, but tell him not to call for a couple of months," I said. I still had radiation to go. This guy Mark must be really evolved to be attracted to a cancer patient, I thought. Here was proof that cancer couldn't stop me. I had triumphed, I'd attracted a nice guy. I was too busy congratulating myself on my obvious evolution to notice that all I'd done was slide down into my old, faulty logic. I was back to thinking of men as symbols—of validation, or resolution, or salvation. I was fleeing the bed, for the bed. And if I hadn't been preening so hard on the dash, I might have questioned this man's attraction to me, or mine to him.

In my rush to be part of a couple—the symbol that everything had turned out just fine—I neglected to ask, But do I like him? If I had, the answer would have been no. Physically Mark was squat and troll-like, not my natural type. Emotionally he was smug, given to marveling at his contributions to the field of photojournalism. "I have the kind of job people would sell their parents for," he would announce roughly every other date.

The subject of Mark's parents was a tricky one. They were concentration camp survivors, a fact that, understandably, had influenced his identity. Not always to the most sympathetic end. "I'm not impressed with breast cancer," he informed me. "I grew up with the Holocaust." I felt compassion when he described being roused as a child by his mother's screams from nightmares. But I couldn't help noticing that the toughest decision he himself had ever had to make was whether to ski Aspen or Vail. Or that, quick to be condescending or acidic, he wasn't exactly the nice guy I'd assumed.

If he wasn't really my type, however, I was, unfortunately, his. Through conversations, I pieced together that Mark had a habit of going after women who'd been traumatized. One girlfriend had watched her father's plane crash into flames. Another had been mugged right before they met. By targeting the walking wounded, maybe he was trying to re-create his role as the family golden boy, but I didn't stick around long enough to say for sure. Once it became clear that he was interested in me not despite the breast cancer but because of it, I was in flight again. My disease, it seemed, had pulled in a diseased person.

The breakup was hard. I didn't miss the man; it was a relief to have him gone. But I was ravenous for security.

I'd also been trying to cut the cancer down to size, to make it into an episode. Episodes are finite. They have conclusions. I'd tried to write Mark in, to make him the happy ending. Well, what kind of ending was this: cancer patient emerges triumphant from treatment, then gets involved with a big fat jerk? I blamed him for ruining the story.

And that's all I wanted right then: triumphant emergence. I wanted to see myself as having somersaulted out of Cancerland to stand tall and victorious: ta-da! More than that, I wanted to cement the exits, seal them shut. But I couldn't. Apparitions of the illness kept slipping out.

I took a trip to the Caribbean. In the gentle light of Virgin Gorda, I thought I'd found escape. The first few mornings were sweet. Rising before the heat, I ran on a path that cut through swarms of yellow butterflies, that nose-dived down into thick, jungly overgrowth. The tangled vegetation was still wet with dew. It brushed my thighs as I ran past, a lazy reminder of regeneration. Grass fringed the path as it started to climb, a gradual rise till it stopped at the edge of a cliff, just before spilling into the ocean. High up, the sun liquefied into air. Below, the sea was azure. The waters beckoned like a promise and I ached to charge ahead, to feel the air rush my legs as I plunged into free fall. Instead I stopped, and caught my breath, and bathed in the lotion of the heat. Each clap of the waves made me punch-drunk with joy.

Inebriation was short-lived. The apparitions found me. They crept up from the side at the beach. Rubbing in sunscreen, I was puzzled to notice navy flecks in the skin on my chest. Blackheads, maybe—I tried to poke one out with a fingernail, but all that happened was I made a dent. When memory revived and I knew what they were, I dropped my hand. The flecks were radiation tattoos. They were the mapping points that had told the technicians where to aim the beam.

I lay back on the towel, cocked one arm overhead, and tried not to look or think. The effort was pointless. Once my eyes were closed, I was in the green radiation room. I remembered how, the first day, they'd laid me down on a soft plastic bed for an hour till it hardened, creating a mold of my body. I remembered the woman who'd settled me into the mold each afternoon. She was large, and kind. Once the machine flashed on, she'd have to scurry into the other room, to avoid the rays. But before and after, we'd talk about our lives. She told me her first husband had been a bastard and the second was her true love, but he'd died.

When we ran out of things to say about marriage, she explained the inner workings of the radiology department. They brought the sickest patients down last, at four o'clock, she said. "When they're on morphine, they sometimes thrash and that makes it hard," she said. "But by the end of the day, they're too exhausted to move." My appointment was at three-thirty. That was cutting it close to the line.

One day when I went she wasn't there. The technicians had gone out on strike. But the patients couldn't just knock off for a week or so while the union worked things out. They had to keep at it or the treatment wouldn't take. The hospital solved the problem by getting the doctors to run the machines. On the first day, the radiologists crowded into the room, chortling nervously about this breach of hierarchy. "It's like the captain of the Concorde flying a commuter plane," a doctor explained to me, in case I didn't get it. I did. I also got the idea that the captains were bamboozled by the controls. "Is this the one you're supposed to use?" I heard one ask, making me afraid that they were going to broil me. With the radiologists in the cockpit, my half-hour daily appointments began taking an hour. I wished the technicians would settle.

On the beach, I kept my eyes closed. I reflected on how the doctors' presence had made me feel, in one respect, like Eve. Until they'd appeared, I hadn't been aware that I was laid out half naked, one arm thrust back over my head, in a parody of a naughty pose. Exactly, I saw with embarrassment, the way I was stretched out now. I yanked my arm down to my side.

A few nights later at dinner, that same arm started to throb. By the time I returned to my cottage, the arm had swollen so large, a silver bracelet was now trapped in the flesh. If I'd been a crying woman, I would have started to sob, for I knew exactly what I had: lymphodema, a side effect of the lymph node dissection, a condition that's largely untreatable. It took an hour to ease the bracelet off. The next day, the ache wasn't so bad, but my lumpy new asymmetry really bothered me. It was weird to be walking around with an arm that looked like it belonged to another person—a person who, unfortunately, weighed a hundred pounds more.

In New York I phoned around. Surely something could be done. I found a company that made lymphodema pumps—a thousand dollars each, but insurance paid. I bought one and brought it home. The pump made a snuffling sound as each compartment of its sleeve filled with air. I was supposed to keep my arm in the sleeve for four hours a day, which worked out to two hours before work, two hours in the evening. My social life was just getting up and running again; now it ground to a halt. I tried to comply with the saleswoman's instructions to the letter. She'd told me to sleep with my arm elevated. I couldn't figure out how, till I hit on the idea of tying my arm to the bedpost with a string. By one or two in the morning, I'd have to cut myself down. I couldn't sleep. I made sure to set the alarm for six anyway, to get two hours' pump time in before work.

One month later I checked my arm carefully. The device hadn't forced the swelling down. My arm looked just the same. I unhooked the sleeve, laid the contraption in its box, and slid it under my bed.

For by now I'd found a bed, a real one, a high and shining brass beauty. As soon as I was able, I threw out the single mattress and launched into an apartment-shopping frenzy. I busted up my savings buying French and Korean antiques and fine black imported sheets with bright orange poppies on them. Only in the dimmest part of my mind did I admit what I was really up to: I was making the apartment as lovely as it could be, in case I had to be laid up at home again. I was decorating my possible next sick rooms.

I made shopping excursions over long lunch hours. I had time—the pace hadn't picked up at work. My proposals still went unanswered. I continued to pretend to be busy when the editor collected the rest of the staff for lunch. I got my hopes up one time, on the day I came to work unveiled—a buzz cut, yes, but hair. "All right!" He grinned. "You look great!" I grinned, too. I was better, he could see that. Now, finally, we could get going. But we didn't. It was as if I'd made one of those terrible first impressions from which you never recover. I'd gotten off to a bad start.

We hardly spoke again till a few months later, when he called me in for a performance review. "Sit down," he said gruffly. He didn't look like a man who wanted to talk. He looked like a man who was under orders from Personnel to deliver the corporate report cards.

"I don't know what to say to you," he began. "I can't review your work. You haven't done much this year. I haven't wanted to give you things to do. Partly for humanitarian reasons. But partly because I wanted to be sure that they got done."

But they would have, I assured him. And you can begin now, I said. Smiling, he said he would. "You know," he chortled. "I really felt bad for you. No one here wanted anything to do with you because you reminded them they could die."

He beamed, as if we were finally sharing the joke. My cheeks burned. *That's* what people thought? On the way out, a buzz in my head made me dizzy, as embarrassment gave way to fear. The editor had fired people for lighter infractions than being walking reminders of death. Without insurance, I was cooked. I had better shape up, although I wasn't sure how. I could try never being out sick again, no matter what. I could start using makeup again, put on the blush. I could get some muscle tone, fake an interest in going to the gym.

I could be profoundly indebted when the magazine's grooming editor passed on a comped invite to a spa. In Utah they got us up at five A.M. and hiked us through red-rock canyons. They trained us in aerobics, in the finer points of low fat, and even though a couple of us busted out for pizza once, I returned five pounds lighter, the blooming picture of health. I was looking good—no one could call me a reminder—and then I blew it. The producer for an afternoon talk show called. They were doing a segment on young women who'd had breast cancer. A local organization where I'd attended a support group had passed along my name. Would I go on? At the time, there'd been hardly any publicity about the fact that women under thirty-five contracted the disease. I knew the last thing I should do if I wanted to clear my record at work was to go on TV with the words "Cancer Victim" emblazoned across my chest. But I remembered the doctor who'd blown me off. After a few days, I phoned back and said yes.

On the day of the broadcast, I gathered with the three other guests in the green room. One announced her profession and the rest of us started. She was a cancer researcher. Another was bald. I was fascinated. This was the first woman I'd ever seen without hair. Lisa was beautiful, which didn't hurt, but still—she was going on TV like that. Clearly this was not someone who was cowering at work, trying to placate some late-middle-aged guy's fears.

Onstage, I took the chair next to her. In the monitor, I noticed that Lisa's back was straight. I sat up, too. A red light flashed. We told our stories. "All right," a man offstage said. The red light went out.

"She doesn't like me," Lisa said to me when the host got up during the break. "She doesn't like it that I came on her show bald." I didn't think she was imagining things. The host was a comedienne who was famous for her shtick and, most recently, for the fact that they'd canceled her celebrity-heavy, late-night show after only one season. She leaned toward the famous, not toward social issues. In her cosmology, talking with cancer patients in the afternoon ranked several levels below schmoozing Arnold and Goldie at night.

The light blinked back on. The host gave it a try, peppered us with questions. Yes, we told her, we had been surprised. No, our doctors, in almost every case, had not believed us. Yes, we were young, that was for sure. At the next break, I expected her to jump up again. Instead she leaned forward, as if to divulge a confidence.

"Plastic surgery, girls," she said inexplicably, in a husky voice. "I'm not kidding you! Plastic surgery, girls—I'm telling you. It's the only way." We glanced at one another. We didn't know what to say. Plastic surgery? Half of her stage guests had just had their breasts done, involuntarily, from scratch. Two of the women smiled politely. Lisa rolled her eyes at me, snorted, giggled. *No way!*

In the green room, we exchanged numbers. Lisa lived three blocks away. We struck up a friendship, and over dinners, she'd casually relate episodes that would have sent me to bed for a week.

"So, the first time I was sick, I met this guy at a party," she said, reaching for the butter, not especially concerned about the twenty pounds she'd gained during treatment. "He's a real Italian stallion, he starts coming on strong. I'm standing there in a wig, no breasts, but the guy doesn't notice. In fact, he wants to go up on the roof, fool around. I thought, Sure. Why not? We go up, we start making out, he runs his hands through my hair. And my hair comes off in his hands."

She was laughing so hard, her eyes squeezed shut. Mine were wide open.

"You know what he did?" she said. "He just stood up slowly and he left. The guy never even said one word."

Lisa was a kick-ass cancer patient, the first of a number I've met. Lisa wasn't one of Bernie Siegel's ECaPs. She was a KACaP. She didn't say, "Try me." She said, "Oh, yeah? Try this."

Like a lot of kick-ass patients, she was younger, weaned on feminism, rock and roll, and self-assertion training. She was a tough babe, who'd gotten tougher still since becoming sick. Though twenty-nine and on her second run with the disease, she wasn't going nowhere gently, and especially not because some doctor told her to. Lisa was the one who told me she stayed in New York because there were more doctors there to fire.

Kick-ass breast cancer patients have done a lot to change the landscape of the illness, external and internal. They're the women you read about in the news, the ones who sue insurance companies that refuse to pay for promising new treatments. They're the ones like Laura's friend Margaret, who, despite being gravely ill, wanted to visit India one more time. She went. Alone.

The generation that is coming into the cancer years now is used to being independent, to fighting for themselves and for causes. Taking their cues from AIDS activists, they've agitated, through organizations like the National Alliance of Breast Cancer Organizations and the National Breast Cancer Coalition and the Susan G. Komen Foundation, for more funding, and they've gotten it: The monies allotted for breast cancer research tripled between 1992 and 1996. By one estimate, the breast cancer groups raised $220 million in four years. And their good fight is paying off beyond cash. Suddenly, after years when the only approach to cancer was, in surgeon Susan Love's words, to slash and burn, so many new treatments are on the horizon, oncologists need special symposiums to keep them straight.

Word is, the cure for cancer is only a few years off. I'll believe it when it's here. But if the cure is close, then credit is due in part to women like these. They only took breast cancer lying down on days when they had to.

Lisa married John, a film producer she met while she was on chemo, and moved back home, to California. "Always send a man to Bendel's for your underwear," she advised me the last time we met. "That way, you know you'll like what he gets." Somehow I think she's fine.

By the time I went on the talk show, my hair was, if not long, luxuriant, startlingly thick and curly. Before, it had been limp and straight. It had never attracted notice. At my sister's wedding, it was a source of constant comment. In New York, strangers approached me to remark on it. At a screenwriting course I'd enrolled in, a famous feminist writer asked where I'd gone to get my hair cut like that. "Beth Israel," I told everyone I'd said. Of course, I hadn't.

I was going to write a screenplay. I was going to write a novel. I was going to do big things and put that whole damn time behind me. I edged away when I ran into women who clung to the disease after it ended. In the support groups I'd been frequenting, I'd seen a couple who couldn't let go of the exemptions it provided. They were flailing, hungering still for the benefits of the illness but unable to reproduce them on their own.

"You can't get a boyfriend if you have cancer," a woman at one group said. "They won't go near you." She seemed bitter and lonely. But she didn't look sick. "When did you have it?" I asked. "Ten years ago," she said, and the answer made me sad. Ten years! For a decade, she'd been hanging out at support groups, blaming cancer for her loveless state. She hadn't fled the bed; she'd stayed burrowed down. But the result was the same: She was stuck.

Some people slip into their disease. It becomes their identity, their covering. "I am an inspiration to all my friends," a neighbor on chemo said the first time we met. She was not doing well. She wore dark glasses all the time and needed a cane to make it to the mailbox. I understood why she made the remark. She was desperate to find meaning in her illness. But I couldn't imagine saying that; it seemed dangerous to voice your investment in calamity.

The majority of women I've known who've gotten cancer have met it with dignity and strength. Kim, the doll-like, blond football queen I first knew in high school, got sick right after her husband left her with two young sons, in Hawaii, where they'd moved for his job. She'd been so delicate, I was afraid she'd crumble. She didn't. She did what was required. She moved to Knoxville, her parents' adopted town, where she knew no one but would have help. Throughout chemo, she worked, as a dental hygienist, and she knocked the disease once. It returned three years later, following another miserable romantic split; after quietly making arrangements for her sons' future, she continued on with her job and life, for a long time. Even when it went to her throat, sickening her further, causing her to gag, Kim made me laugh each time I called, although once, she said something that left me chilled. "If I'd known bad men were going to kill me," she said, "I'd never have gotten so upset over those guys." Raising two boys on her own, with cancer—she truly was heroic.

Sandra, too, was indomitable. For years after her disease went to the bone, she ran a multinational conglomerate. Even when she had to walk with a cane, she had no interest in taking it easy— or in the illness, particularly, beyond the necessary fight. "I heard you got terrific news," I said when I found myself standing beside her at a party. A mutual friend had just reported that her tumor markers had fallen again. "Yes," she said, staring at me levelly. "My daughter graduated from college." Her doctors gave her a few years, but Sandra took seven, and kicked the disease around a time or two along the way.

Some people are admirably transformed, and some stay the course—hard enough, given its slams and jolts. But some, a few, milk the illness, their own or others'. These are the ones a friend refers to as cancer queens.

Cancer queens demand sympathy. They play on guilt and burn through support. "No one will talk to me anymore," said a woman who called to ask about an herbal treatment she'd heard, through an acquaintance, that I'd tried. This didn't seem like an auspicious opening. "The doctors say I have to do something," she added. "I . . . I just need some support."

What, I asked, was she doing? Was she taking hormones?

"They want me to try Cytadren," she said. "But I read it could hurt your adrenal glands."

Then what about Meges? I asked. I knew people who'd had luck with that one.

"No," she said. "I don't want to get fat." Neither had my friends who'd put on fifteen pounds. But they hadn't wanted to get dead, either.

Nor did she want to try chemo (hair), radiation (fatigue), the herbal drops (cost).

"Maybe I'll just put my affairs in order and die with dignity," she sighed, mimicking the phrase that the press had applied to Jackie Onassis's last days with lymphoma. Death with dignity, I repeated—but what did that mean? She couldn't quite say. How about life with dignity, I argued. You're still alive—fight. But she wouldn't. She began calling three times a week or more, leaving helpless messages. "I just . . . I just need encouragement," she'd say. "My doctors say I have to act." When I'd pick up, we'd have a replay of the first conversation. Her doctors, I suspected, could have used a support group—another idea she vetoed.

In less than a month, I had no patience left, despite the fact that she really did need support. I felt heartless, but like everyone, I turned away. I stopped taking the calls. There was something perverse about the manner in which she made herself out to be a victim while ignoring the ways in which she truly was one. She seemed to want the talk-show version of cancer. It was as if she'd been swept up in the cultural movement that trades in wounds, that rewards all victims equally, genuine and phony.

(On the subject of the phony, there's been a rise in numbers. "More and more people [have been] pretending to be sick so they could join Internet support groups," *The New York Times* reports. In the extreme, feigned illness is called factitious disorder. Marc D. Feldman and Charles V. Ford document extraordinary cases of it in a book called *Patient or Pretender.* After telling his associates that he had cancer, a premed student used masking tape and a sunlamp to create an irritation on his back that he claimed was a radiation spot. "He maintained a high level of interest by telling friends that he was facing critical treatment and went so far as to record farewell messages on tapes 'just in case,'" the authors write, noting that cancer has a particular appeal to factitious patients: "The heroic image that cancer survivors sometimes have is attractive [to them], as is the strong emotional response a cancer diagnosis is sure to draw from loved ones and associates.")

A while ago, a woman I'd worked with once began calling about a friend of hers who had cancer. Though I didn't know the woman well, I was upset by her news. I offered up comfort and called the friend, to see if there was anything I could do. After that, my acquaintance began phoning regularly, with increasingly detailed reports on her friend's decline. Cynthia had vomited on the street. Cynthia's doctors had removed a muscle in her abdomen and now she was unable to sit up. Cynthia's doctors were cruel and unfeeling; one had been mean to her mother. At first I was all sympathy and ears, till I began to notice that in the telling, her suffering was always equal to, or greater than, Cynthia's.

"I'm just—I'm just so upset," she would begin. "I have not been able to sleep all night." Even among people who *had* cancer, I'd never heard someone be this distraught.

"Is Cynthia, like, her best friend?" I asked someone who'd gone to school with the woman.

"I don't think so," she said, sounding puzzled.

The calls started to make me squirm. I began to notice she kept pain scores, and awarded herself top points. "When I was sick, I found it was helpful to—" I'd start. "You weren't sick like this, I don't think. What we're going through is much, much worse," she'd say, although she'd never asked about my illness. In fact, I noticed, she never really asked how I was.

How did you get yourself dragged into the World Cancer Cup? I thought, kicking myself, after another overwrought Cynthia call. Poor Cynthia, but I'd begun to wish she would expire.

"I—I am just so upset," the woman had declared this time. "I mean, I am simply not able to work anymore." Uncrossing my eyes and unsticking my tongue, I'd asked how she was planning to spend the holidays. But she was too quick for a change of subject.

"I will not be *celebrating* New Year's," she said. "Cynthia is sick."

I became busy whenever she called, but a few months later, feeling guilty, I phoned to invite her to an evening I was hosting.

"Cynthia is very bad," she said. I took that as a no.

And what had she been up to? "I have been going to an oncoshrink," she said. "She's been helping." Refraining from inquiring if the therapist had broken the news yet that she was not actually ill, I asked for the woman's name. "I'm writing an essay about cancer," I explained, "and might want to interview her."

The thunderous quiet on the other end was the sound of someone drawing herself up. "I cannot believe," she intoned, the deepest affront in her voice, "that I am telling you this and you bring up your work."

"Listen," I said, patience breaking. "Have you considered that *maybe* I'm not somebody to have lengthy discussions about this with, given my history? Have you thought that maybe it's a little hard for me to hear?"

"This is not the first time you've been insensitive," she snapped. "When I called to tell you Cynthia's cancer had metastasized, you said, 'I hate when that happens.'"

"Bad joke," I apologized, although between two cancer patients it wouldn't have been. I must have forgotten she was only playing at the role. "But when I hear about gruesome treatments, my defenses fly up. I can't take it."

So if you would, please, stuff it, was my point. She didn't get it.

"I am sorry," she said, "but I am not here to help you with your problems. I have *much* too full a plate."

"Cancer queen," two friends with AIDS hooted when I related the conversation. "We call people like that 'mother of the victim' or 'friend of the victim.'"

"Are there AIDS queens?" I asked.

"Oh, honey, yes," one said.

"Oh, absolutely," the other said.

"And some of them even have AIDS."

CHANGE

AROUND THE TIME PEOPLE STOPPED SAYING, "YOU LOOK great!," maybe fourteen months after chemo, I had a scare. Two nights before my thirty-fifth birthday, I attempted a breast exam, my first; the discovery of the pigeon's egg had been accidental. Tiny lumps were everywhere, scatterings of small, hard beans. I didn't know this was how most breasts are, ripply, not Barbie smooth. I thought the cancer was back and was eating me alive. I thought I was dying.

I got up and poured a huge drink. Its warmth calmed me and I fell asleep, but the next day, a Saturday, I was up and jangled by five. In the tattered light of dawn I wandered the apartment, lifting a book to put it away, then absently setting it down. At a decent hour, I left to run errands, but in the supermarket the cart made me furious. It was goddamn wobbly. I shoved it away. Across the street and back upstairs, I made myself look up Bonner's number. "Tell him I need him to schedule a mammogram right away," I said when the service answered. "And tell him I need Valium."

The Valium was a mistake. At times in the past, it had been my mainstay, my comfort, but now its molecular structure rearranged mine. It master-force-10 blasted me. My system, high strung enough to have once tried to commit seppuku over pond water, went hysterical as the Valium produced what is called a paradoxical, or reverse, drug reaction: I didn't calm down, I revved up. I got manic.

Ten milligrams each morning, and I was out, in high flight, glam-packed and lofted on air. In the subway, I jumped a turnstile. I bought a metal World War I French army helmet and wore it around, God knows why. I couldn't sleep and took to guzzling Scotch, which further scrambled my brains. Late at night, watching MTV, I was privy to the secret truths encoded in Luther Vandross videos. I began arriving at the office at five A.M., the better to work on the book proposal I was feverishly dashing off. I took time from the proposal to compose frenzied letters. I sent one to a former boss. I don't know what I said, but she avoided my calls for years. I sent another to my sister and received one in reply. "I can't help you by mail," she wrote. "Phil says you're just being an asshole."

I was so crazy, I didn't know anything was wrong. But the editor did. After two weeks of watching my behavior get loopier, he called me into his office.

"Have a seat," he said, eyeing me cautiously. "I don't know what's the matter with you. You're not acting normal. I think you're on the verge of a nervous breakdown. The whole time you were sick, you were walking around here like a tight-assed WASP. It's catching up with you." Employee Assistance wanted to talk with me. He handed me the number.

The Employee Assistance woman was understanding when I described my situation. I told her about the cancer, confided I'd found lumps and was scared, explained I was waiting for a mammogram. That must be really hard, she said sympathetically. Must be a lot of pressure. But maybe you need to talk to a shrink. I said I would.

I didn't tell her about the tranquilizers or Scotch; I didn't think to. I had no idea they were making me whacked till I had the test and it came back fine and I threw out the rest of the prescription.

Within two days, the mania lifted. Clarity returned and I saw how I'd behaved. I was mortified. I would have traded my new apartment, anything, to go back and erase the incident. Since I couldn't, I made a decision: I would never take another drink or unnecessary drug again. I couldn't risk it. The incident scared me so bad that so far, I haven't.

My two-week excursion to the outer-sanity boroughs didn't boost my standing at the magazine. I thought about requesting a meeting. I mean, I could explain. The whole thing was a mistake, it was the Valium, give me one more chance, I would try harder. But from the way the editor stared through me in the hall, it was clear he didn't want to hear any explanations. From the expression on his face, I guessed he'd suspected I was going to pull a stunt like this ever since that hair-loss maneuver. It looked like my days were numbered.

Now I sent through story proposals just to buy time. Insurance was crucial. I could not be without a job, without benefits. But a recession was on, magazines were folding. Everyone said there were no jobs.

As a clemency gambit, I kept my appointment with the shrink Employee Assistance recommended, a psychotherapist named George Neden. We discussed my recent past, beginning with the disease. "I got breakup cancer," I said, for I'd become convinced that's what it was. I'd seen a lot of it around support groups, I told him: woman goes through a split, then, *wham*, finds a lump. He didn't agree. What I was seeing was coincidence, he said. Wasn't it true that breast cancer took years to reach a detectable size? How could it just pop up overnight? He concluded that my best next move would be to fall in love, find happiness with a man, sort of get back on the horse.

After the events of the last few years, after the divorce, and Mark, and what I'd being learning of men at the men's magazine, I was in no mood for a boyfriend. "My dating attitude is, You fuck with me, I'll tear your head off," I tried to explain, but added that

I'd try. I did. I didn't get a lot of callbacks. I would go out with someone to appease Neden, then find a reason to snarl at the person. Sometimes I didn't even wait for the date. "Oh yeah, I've really been sitting here sobbing since noon," I told one guy who was trying to apologize for phoning late.

Neden's approach was well-meaning but misconceived. "You don't understand," I said one week. "I've lost too much. I can't want anything, or anyone, anymore. During chemo, I cut myself off, and now I can't come back to life."

A month later, I countered with another obstacle.

"You don't understand," I said. "I know the cancer's coming back. It's like I'm on the floor at McDonald's and the gunman's still in the building. I can sense it. It's still around." I snuck a look at Neden's face. Sixth senses were suspect in therapy; I had to know if he would cut me slack and take mine seriously. Bonner hadn't, on my last visit. You're cured, he'd told me, smiling broadly when I told him I had a bad feeling. Go home and don't worry. You're cured. But at home I was even more uneasy. Instinct didn't care that I'd just been officially declared cured. Instinct was pricking me, buzzing in a low-current hum that produced the thought: The illness is coming back; it's only a matter of time. If the cancer existed in my psyche, did that mean it was all in my mind? Or did it mean that it still existed, in some form? Would that form eventually be realized—was I onto something Bonner didn't want to see?

To Neden's credit, he didn't insist that I was all fine now. He didn't tell me I was just responding to old fear. "Even if the gunman's there," he said, "you still have to come back to life. In fact, it may be you're already alive." But I couldn't come back. I didn't know how.

He was right, too, on the second score. It took me a while to learn it, but I wasn't really dead inside. After the recent uproar, I had mistaken quiet for emptiness. My life wasn't hollow, it was fallow. It had become like a field in early spring, brown and plain on the surface, teeming with renewal below. I'd wriggled under to be closer to nutrients. I was lying low, and I was growing strong.

Victor and I had a parting of the ways. On a follow-up visit, he was examining my breasts when a petite Asian woman banged open the door. "Get out!" he shouted. She began speaking excitedly, in what might have been pidgin Mandarin. "Get out," he ordered. "Out."

"Jesus," he swore, once she was gone.

"Who was that?" I asked, grabbing my gown shut.

"Oh, my wife," he said. "She has an IQ of two."

"Your wife?" I said. They were married? The woman was not really an English speaker—although that might have been a point they had in common. "How did you meet her?"

"Um, through friends," he answered.

After the appointment, I called Bonner. "Do I have to keep going to that guy?" I asked. "Is it necessary? Can't I just see you?"

One doctor on the case would be enough, Bonner agreed. Fine, he said. No problem. From now on, I could skip Victor.

The main event in my life became the gym. Forty-five minutes on the StairMaster, five times a week. I became a fat-gram zealot. I grew sculpted and lean and my mind returned to fighting trim. Chemo had scorched my concentration. For a time, the sharp truncated intensity of poetry had been all I could manage. But now I slid back into novels, the more dense and complex, the better. In *The Good Soldier* by Ford Maddox Ford, I came across this passage: "If you know anything about breakdowns, you will know that, by the ingenious torments that fate prepares for us, these things come as soon as, a strain having relaxed, there is nothing more to be done. It is after a husband's long illness and death that a widow goes to pieces; it is at the end of a long rowing contest that a crew collapses and lies forward upon its oars." Maybe that's what had happened at the office—I'd fallen on my oars.

In my reading, I returned to the guys I'd loved in college: Paul Tillich, Thomas Merton, the best of the twentieth century's theologians. When I remembered to, I prayed.

At first after chemo, I played at prayer. "I need your help," I'd begin, then stop. Who was "you"? I still wasn't sure whom I was addressing. I'd studied so many belief systems, my own had become blenderized. My first religious influence had been my mother, who, in time-honored Episcopalian tradition, didn't seem to have it quite straight whether she was attending church or a country club. She was certain, for instance, of our prospect of getting into heaven. "You know they're going to let your great-grandmother in," she reasoned. "And you know she's going to get us all in." We had advance acceptance.

My father's Christian Science wasn't an immediate influence. My dad kept quiet about his beliefs, particularly once my sister and I reached our teenage years, when a silent offense was his best defense. "Hey, did Mary Baker Eddy pay that phone bill yet?" one of us would ask at the dinner table. The joke never failed to make both of us collapse. Each time my father smiled wanly. Yes, it was true that the founder of Christian Science had been buried with a phone in her coffin. No, the line wasn't still connected. He kept his head high even when my sister convinced the neighborhood kids that his church worshiped kitchen appliances. "See?" she said once as my father rushed in the front door and down the hall to greet my mother, who was cooking dinner. "I told you. They have to kiss the toaster as soon as they come home."

Despite the persecution he suffered at home, my father remained the picture of religious tolerance. When I went through my witchcraft stage, he never said a word. After that, I had a casual fling with Buddhism. In college, in my studies, I gave God a more formalized try, but later, in my twenties and otherwise occupied, I abandoned my intellectual efforts. Faith is impossible to defend or describe, so I'll only say that later, when

I wasn't quite looking, I came to believe. Or more accurately, returned to belief. On some level, it had been there all along.

I kept quiet about this. In urban areas, in New York and L.A., it was okay to say you were spiritual. You could even mention "divinity" or "higher power." But it made people edgy if you talked about God. Conversations about sex were fine, but religion was bad form, the provenance of the untutored. Organized religion, in some circles, was still the opiate, was claptrap; near brushes with death were no excuse to indulge. I'd never had a problem with organized religion as I knew it; the Episcopalians and their forefathers had stayed out of the Inquisition and allegiances with the CIA. I believed, but I shut up about it.

Through prayer, I sometimes entered a numinous state, and that was a fortunate thing. In the days ahead, that's precisely where I'd need to be.

Thirty-five was winding down. I looked for a job and tried to hold on to the one I had. I worked out. I spent hours in restaurants; I'd acquired some new friends. Some nights I went to parties.

At a gathering in a bar, I made a stupid mistake. Bored and not drinking, I bummed a cigarette. Just one, I promised myself, though I knew these were sucker words. Soon I was ducking into the lobby of the Roosevelt Hotel for a couple of lunchtime smokes. The only people who went there were down on their luck, which, if you subscribe to the theory that you make your own, by then included me. An ex–cancer patient smoking—how embarrassing. I hid out where no one would see me. I blew my cover, so to speak, one night at a party, when a nicotine fit drove me to beg a cigarette from my friend Joe. "Uh, weren't you just seriously ill?" he asked, hand poised over his jacket pocket.

Within three months, I was hooked, keeping it down to five or ten a day, but flat-out hooked, and I stayed hooked even after the disease came back, until finally my luck turned again and an acupuncturist rid me of the addiction. My luck didn't just move of its own accord, though. It took three years of trying before I could quit, and in that time I assumed I was the only oncology patient fool enough to smoke. But, of course, I wasn't.

"Yes, you told me to bring the prescription. Well, I didn't. Well, I'm sorry. Well, I left it at home, okay?" I could hear the guy through the curtain at the Sloan Kettering Cancer Center emergency room. This was years later, and I was in for a mild complaint, a banged shoulder that needed an X ray. He was there with his mother, who, it was obvious, was driving him nuts.

"I have to go to the bathroom," he said. "If the nurse comes, you talk to her."

The son was still gone when the nurse arrived. The mother sounded happy to take charge. Forty-three, she answered crisply. Yes, lung. No, not anymore. No, he quit. About six months ago. They were just starting in on insurance when a commotion at the end of the room interrupted them. "Hey!" the head nurse called out. "What's that? Who's smoking in the bathroom?"

I once had occasion to spend time on Dilaudid, a synthetic form of heroin, and I once did a run on morphine. As a subsequent specialist in quitting, I can testify that it's true what they say: Heroin—morphine, too—is easier to give up than cigarettes. Nicotine is fiercer than threat or reason, a fact that explains the bald wretches who huddle on the Sloan Kettering doorstep, one hand around an IV pole, the other holding a cigarette. It's a startling sight, but then again, where else are you going to find smokers these days?

Thirty-six squeaked closer. My life was schizoid. I secretly smoked/I ran before work. The resulting glow (or maybe it was the bad dating attitude) attracted the interest of numerous men/they all left me cold. After hours I was cresting on a joy that had begun to take hold/on the job I was miserable. The editor killed the women's essay columns. In the hall he no longer looked through me, but away. I figured I had days. I was right.

"Close the door," the editor said, glancing up from a manuscript. "Have you spoken with Personnel?"

I had. They were giving me an extra month to look. But they weren't giving me any reason.

"Why am I being fired?" I asked.

"I don't know," the editor said, looking at me hard. "Why do you think?"

I shrugged to signal that if he didn't know, neither did I.

"Do you realize that by firing me, you could be leaving me without insurance?" I asked. I wanted this spelled out.

He nodded.

"Do you realize that if my cancer came back, it could bankrupt me and my family?"

He nodded again.

"And you don't care?"

He shook his head slowly. No.

What more was there to say? I was out, first of the year.

In the months after, messengers came with my files. I pushed them under the bed, next to the pump. Letters arrived, forwarded from the office. One was from a writer I liked. "Where are you? How are you? I'm worried about you," he wrote. I didn't respond. How was I going to say where I'd gone?

Mostly I spent the days in a green swivel chair, staring at the bookshelf and overcoming my resistance to tears. I made a scientific study of them. Crying was release, I noted, a remedial emotional anthropologist. It just seemed in the build as if it might smash you. But it could only pound you if you refused to give in. It was only when you held back that you got shaky.

———————

In early spring, a former colleague called. The editor had submitted two of my pieces together with a third and had gotten his first National Magazine Award nomination.

On the subway, a burly guy asked for change. "I'm looking for work," he said.

"Me, too!" I exclaimed. "I don't have a job either."

"Well, at least you have your health," he said, backing off.

"Actually, that's not true!" I said, on a roll. "I had cancer."

"Well, everyone's got problems," he said snappishly, and walked away.

Emotional exhaustion put me into a stupor. I was apathetic, dimmed. Now that I'd learned to cry, I couldn't stop. "You sound like you're on the edge," Joe said, and he was right. I was; on the edge of nothing. I didn't like to leave the apartment. I was scared of people, scared to have them look at me. Shrouded in unhappiness, unemployed, I slipped back into the old mantra. Divorce, cancer, pariah-hood on the job—I replayed my tragedies till I was tired of them, till I felt like I'd taken them up the nose. I was sick of being indebted to tragedy for definition, of regarding it as predictive. I decided to become my own psychic, make my own forecasts. Wouldn't it be funny, I thought, if I actually kept on going? They'd be amazed. I wasn't sure who "they" were. But one Monday in June, I felt something sing within me, some universal harmony. It occurred to me that I was glad to be alive, glad to be who and where I was.

I began spending less time in the chair. Jobs were coming my way. Part-time work. A fashion designer who wanted his own publication installed me and another editor in the basement of his townhouse to work on a prototype. My fellow staff member was a beauty editor, also between magazines. We were the sixth team he'd tried in the last five years. For two months, we wrote fake headlines no one saw for fake stories no one liked, till the designer lost interest and replaced us with another fake staff.

A celebrity weekly hired me to fill in for vacationing writers. They started me out on deep captions. Though this wasn't exactly elevated work, I took it as a good sign. My life was curving forward, like a scimitar. I wasn't even fazed when one of the senior writers, a man I'd once had dinner with, stopped by to smirk. "It's really unprecedented for someone with your background, who's worked at"—and he stated my credentials—"to be writing copy blocks at this magazine," he said. "I mean, for someone with ten, twelve, fifteen years' experience to end up in the pits of this company, in a job that's only ever been held by people much younger, people right out of school, it's astonishing. Not to be disparaging," he added, smiling. I smiled right back. It wasn't every day I had the benefit of a career assessment from the author of the Linda Evans diet book. Who cared what the guy thought? Maybe I'd been reading too much New Age, but I'd begun to see that each new situation was valuable for its lessons. And I was learning on this job.

"We need a three-page story on her by tomorrow," someone would say, thwacking a stack of files on the desk. The tower would make me queasy: a complete article by the next day? I'd always been a slow and skittish writer. One sentence might take hours. But though at first each story would provoke a meltdown—what if I couldn't write it and they had to publish blank pages?—the high-speed pace of the weekly forced me to become more fluid. Soon I began taking other freelance writing jobs. Up till then, I'd been all talk on the subject of writing—sure, I could write, if I wanted to—but beyond a couple of travel pieces, I'd never tested the assumption. Now editors were calling back with second assignments. I wasn't entirely sure I hadn't just fooled them the first time. But even if that was so, I was grateful to learn I could bluff.

"I'm coming back to life," I told myself. "It's been four years since the divorce, but I'm coming back to life. I'm graduating from tragedy." Some afternoons, I'd walk through Barneys and imagine all the things I was going to buy when I got a real job. At night I imagined a man in bed with me, a man who'd be kind, a man I could hold.

In late fall, I broke off a twisty friendship I'd been in with a man named Ben, a magazine writer ten years older. When we first met, about the time I'd ended it with Mark, I'd been half in love. But the guy had been all flirtation, no action, for years, and I was tired of being bogged down in promise. The relationship was always on the verge of blossoming. Ben had become a stand-in for a boyfriend. I was, I admitted to myself, hanging out with him in lieu of the real thing. I cut loose just before Thanksgiving.

The weekly kept asking me back. I kept getting outside assignments, and now a publisher had approached me about writing a book, a quickie, three-month-turnaround project, not prestigious, but a book. They wanted to see a proposal. I didn't see how I could. By fall, a deep exhaustion had settled into my bones, suckling so hard, my hands sometimes trembled, leaving me near tears at the thought of even attempting a book. I'd first noticed that my energy was slipping in August—after a one-week stint at the magazine, I was unable to get out of bed till noon for two days. But I was slaving like a maniac and I'd aced a checkup in June and besides, what was I expected to do: grow frantic over every twinge, even if, true, the twinges were mounting? Other than a tiredness that occasionally made me trip, however, nothing suggested that an early visit to the oncologist's was in order. No, my complaints, while annoying, were fairly ordinary: one stun-gun headache that lasted three days, repeat fevers, a scratchy throat, laryngitis a month on. (It was only in retrospect that I questioned whether this cluster wasn't a warning that my immune system was sparking out.) That, and a bad back, my first. "Your father has one, too," my mother said, which surprised me. I'd never heard him mention pain so strong, it could turn you pale. Then again, given his denomination, he wouldn't.

On the morning of a job interview, I pressed on my spine and set off a burning ripple that sent me flying to the floor. At the interview, the editor and I compared back stories. He was a fellow sufferer.

A friend offered the name of a chiropractor. "It's great when he cracks your back," she said. "Don't worry. It doesn't really hurt." She was wrong. It was horrid; it made me moan. Nonetheless, I was devoted in my attendance. I needed to get in shape because not one, not two, but four job offers had come in. The lessons of my last full-time job weren't lost on me: I picked the magazine that appeared to have the highest sanity level. It was also, fortunately, one I liked to read—a quirky women's glossy, funny and smart. I said I'd start after the New Year. I had a couple of things I had to do.

I needed to buy me a bathing suit; my family was spending Christmas in Puerto Vallarta. I needed to finish an article. And I needed to gather up my medical paperwork. I'd decided to change oncologists.

In the years after, my memory edited out the details of this time. The move to a new doctor, for instance, was remade in my mind as a perfunctory piece of business: I was changing jobs, so I changed oncologists, too—too many bad associations with the old one. I made an appointment with a friend's, a woman called Dr. Susan Kruze, and she ordered up the standard round of introductory scans and tests, and I went off to Mexico. I just kind of switched, no big deal.

But the accounting, as I tend to remember it, is so skeletal as to be inaccurate. It's not what really happened. Recently, while delving through a journal from that year, I was floored to come upon this entry, from immediately after I'd met with Kruze:

12/17. Went to see Neden. I was venting frustrations about the upcoming tests ("But I don't want any more needles!") when I noticed his mood was so dark, it was infecting the room. He was tense, almost angry, and then I realized—he's really upset. Two weeks ago, I remembered, I'd told him, "I have this fear my cancer is back. Last time I was sick, I had this odd feeling in my molars, and now my teeth feel the same way again." But deep down, my instincts tell me I'll be fine, I wanted to assure him. He looked so helpless and concerned that I felt guilty, like I'd been scaring him on purpose. Like I'd done something wrong, hurt him somehow.

It was the first time ever I've felt, on a gut level, how I mattered to another human being, was aware I had a real impact on someone. I felt compassion for his fear and anger, knew that it mattered to one person that I be well and live. He was truly upset and would be worried about me this weekend.

It was a profound hour. My will to fight for my life started to return. Any ambivalence left about living was knocked out of me. I would live and I wanted to live. My spirit returned to my body. My time on earth began again. My soul's work was starting. I was lighter.

I knew. But how did I know? Molars? There's no mention of a molar connection in any of the oncological journals. And was it really that pat: One person cared about me, I felt it on a soul level, and *bam*, I made the decision to come back to life, to fight? But there it is, all laid out—the warning and the healing, the eventual resolution and salvation.

Nor is this the only warning I found. Signal lights flash from every third or fourth page of that journal, horribly chilling now, in retrospect.

There is, for instance, this dream:

Danger's coming. Claire [a woman I knew who'd had cancer] hands me a gun with a nuclear explosion device. I blow a hole in the ceiling. We start to run. A firestorm's coming, everyone's running from the unnamed danger. Fear isn't pumping through me, though. I kind of know I'll make it.

And far more ominous, from a few weeks earlier, this one:

I'm in a low, wide bamboo tunnel, rushing to keep up with Lynn [my friend from college]. She's motioning me on; we're giddy and tumbling—girly, the way we'd been in Europe. Lynn's laughing, and I think how odd it is that she's walking me through what appears to be an exotic museum; she's never had patience for museums. As my eyes adjust to the dim, slatted light, however, I see we aren't in an art gallery at all, but in a menagerie of death. Lynn doesn't notice, or she doesn't mind. "Now, that's my kind of exhibit," she shrieks, plopping herself onto a sarcophagus, a mummy casing, made of rice. Brushing herself off, she clambers ahead, high-spirited, reflecting on her life: ". . . and then I moved to New York with this woman, and she got married to an Argentine, and after her marriage broke up, she got sick," she says, and just as it dawns on me that she's describing me, another realization hits: "Lynn," I think. "You're dead." I say nothing, but she looks at me and nods and she's no longer my giggly friend. She is somber, an apparition, my guide through the museum of death. We shuffle on in silence, crossing into a dark tight part of the tunnel, where we're joined by a black man in blue pajamas. "I'm a prisoner here," he says. "But sometimes I escape. I go to Livonia," and suddenly, they both turn and fly through a side door, leaving me alone. "Wait!" I shout, racing after them. Coming into sunlight, I blink. I'm in some kind of Celebration City, a grassy stage-lot suburbia, beside a benchful of old men. "Have you seen them?" I cry. The old men just stare. Before me, a road crosses my footpath. I could go in either direction. "Do you know how to get to—" I start to ask, then stop. I can't remember the name of the place where Lynn and I began.

I remember waking from that dream into a musty gray light, terrified, heart skidding painfully low in my chest. Some of the individual images mystified me, but I had no doubt what, collectively, they meant.

The dream was clearly telling me the cancer was coming back.

And so I was stunned but not shocked when one week into the new job, three weeks after the bone scan, I got a call from the new oncologist. "I don't want you to wait for the mammogram," she said, voice urgent and low. "I think you'd better come right in."

SPURS

ALL OVER. THE BONE SCAN WAS SHOWING SOMETHING all over.

"I'm seeing abnormalities everywhere," Kruze was saying. "I'm very concerned." It was my second Friday of the new job, the first payday. I'd been there a week and a half.

Abnormalities? I knew she was hedging, trying to stall questions. I knew she didn't want to have this conversation on the phone. But my mind seized on the loophole she'd presented. Abnormalities, I repeated—couldn't that be arthritis? I had arthritis—did she know that? My mother and I, we both had arthritis. And arthritis, she had to know, could show up on a scan.

Well, couldn't it?

"It's a very remote possibility," she conceded, and what I heard was the word *possibility*. She couldn't say more till she saw the X rays, and Radiology didn't have an opening until Monday. Stop by then, she told me. She'd leave an envelope with requisition slips at the desk.

As I was writing down directions, my eye fell on the date: January 15. It was ten years exactly to the day of my wedding, and I was learning I was in sickness once more, that my cancer was probably back.

My office was quiet. I really have to do something about this avalanche on my desk, I thought after a minute, pulling a white sheet at random from the pile. The words on it were straight black tracks. My eyes slid across them, again and again. Twenty minutes later, or maybe two hours, I placed a call to Claire, a friend who'd also had breast cancer, the person who'd recommended this oncologist. Sorrow was making my tongue leaden. Depression curdled in my chest, sadness weighed like an anchor in my belly. I would only be able to tell one person that day. Otherwise, I might crack apart.

"Remember what you said when I got sick?" Claire said after a pause. She was speaking in the bright, peppy clip she fell into when she was uneasy. "You said, 'Cancer is not a death sentence.' Let me remind you of that: This is not a death sentence."

Oh, no? I thought. "Once breast cancer's come back, they'll never say you're cured," I remembered Lisa telling me two and a half years before, and the relief I'd felt at not being in that limbo. Only six months before, Bonner had said exactly that to me: Cured.

Ear to the phone, I sketched arrows and the few random words of Claire's that were able to penetrate my brain: "Tamoxifen," "lived for years." My fingers on the pencil were still brown from Mexico. Four drooping tulips from the new-job bouquets were still in a vase on my desk. Their cards were in an adjacent pencil holder. "Congratulations!" they read. And, "They're lucky to have you!" All around was evidence that my life was continuing its bright curve forward. Invitations to screenings were spread out in front of me. Clips for stories I wanted to assign were stacked nearby. And an office with two windows and a long black sofa—those were tangible signs of forward motion. I had visual proof—I could not be returning, I could not be sliding back down into Cancerland.

Suddenly I realized: I wasn't. Cancer wasn't dragging me back into its world, that's not what was happening. Cancer didn't have to. It had smashed through the final barriers, busted through permanently into mine. It had been waiting patiently here, in my fine new office, that morning. It would slither through the apartment door ahead of me that night. From now on, cancer would be there, biding its time. And mine.

"Do you want me to call Ben?" Claire asked.

"Yeah, why not," I said. What did it matter if there wasn't clarity between us, if the undercurrents were murky? Ben could be a fierce ally, a strong friend, when he wanted to, and I knew he would.

By the weekend, normal time cycles vanished. No night, no day, only dense, perpetual present. In bed and on the street, my thoughts ran together in a hum. *I hate thinking of leaving the people I love. I hate that this may be the end of my life. I hate that I didn't make more of a difference to anyone. Thirty-seven. What was the point? Thirty-seven. Here I am, alone and maybe dying. Thirty-seven. How could this be?*

Whatever song had begun within me a month before now deepened into a lament. A car horn would honk and interrupt it, or the managing editor would arrive with galleys and it would fade for a minute, then resume with a different verse. But always, the refrain was the same.

Where in my body is it?

On Saturday a bouquet of flowers arrived, from Ben. On Sunday Claire called. "They're having amazing success with hormones," she said. "You're not going to die." Some hours, I was drowning, clutching at her words. Some hours, I wasn't; no big deal, I would take the hormones, right? I would be okay. Some hours, I knew exactly which bone it was in. The upper left arm, definitely, the cancer was a dull black place near the shoulder, or maybe it was the sharp ache near my knee—if that wasn't from the gym—or, no, more likely, it was the strange sensation in my shin. Yes, absolutely. The shin. There was a feeling like television static in there.

Some hours, I rallied on insight: All you have is the present, I'd coach myself, the same as everyone else—this day, right now. You weren't singled out; you have the same amount of time as every other person: the next twenty-four hours.

On Sunday I kept the promise from December: Forcing myself to leave the apartment, I walked across Seventeenth Street and into Barneys, where I spent my new paycheck on Women's, third floor. Cancer wasn't going to ruin the moment. I'd worked too hard for it. But it was the principle, not the clothes, that I was after. The three black bags stayed unpacked in the hall.

On Monday the hospital was oddly hushed, halls empty. The stillness made me jumpy till I remembered: Martin Luther King Day. On the third floor, Kruze's office was locked, but an envelope with my name was taped to the door. Peeling it off, I started toward the elevator, then checking behind me, stopped in the middle of the long corridor. I couldn't wait. I tore the envelope open.

Seven areas. Oh, Jesus. Seven. All through my spine and ribs. One spot in my calf. Even one in the back of my head. To keep from slumping against a wall, I walked myself in a circle. The cancer was in my skull? What if it grew and broke the skull bone? Seven places, half my skeleton: How was I going to tolerate that much pain? And how long would I have to?

That night I went to Ben's apartment. When he opened the door, his thick eyebrows were knitted and his face was dark. I lay on his couch. He sat in a chair, clicking the remote. We watched slide-show TV.

Two mornings later, at eight A.M., Kruze stood when I was ushered into her office. She was a tall woman, wide-jawed, with the reflexively self-assured air of an MBA. I took a seat. She got to the point.

"I have the X rays back," she said. "I was right. The cancer has spread to the bone."

Hunching into the chair, I pressed a fist against my mouth while she provided an introduction to Stage Four disease. "Breast cancer usually goes to the same places: brain, liver, lungs, bones," she said. "What you have is, technically, breast cancer to the bone. Even when it's spread, it's still breast cancer—it's in your bones, but we use breast cancer drugs to treat it."

In one respect I was fortunate, she said, and I nodded quickly. Whatever it was, I would take it. Fortunate because with spread to the soft organs, the brain, liver, lungs, patients had a shorter life expectancy. "You need your liver to stay alive," she elaborated. "You don't really need your bones." I frowned—I thought I did—but longer was good, that was fine.

"You live longer when the disease is in the bone," she said. "But the bad news is, it's more painful." That was because the cancer could cause fractures—although the way mine was located, she said, we didn't have to worry.

And AIDS patients might get spots on their face. It was later, on a trip to a bookstore, that I discovered how demonic breast-to-the-bone could be. As the tumors began to feed and rampage, they could press on a femur, gently at first, then with violence and force. My bones could be broken from within. My vertebrae might collapse or crumble, my spinal cord become severed. I could lose control of my legs and bowels. Two paragraphs into the advanced chapter, I was sickened. This was the illness turned vicious, the pain Bonner had said didn't come till later on.

"We'll start you out on hormone treatment," Kruze said. "Fifty percent of patients respond. But it will take about four months to know. You can't tell right away if it's working."

And what would happen, in that time, if it didn't?

The cancer could spread again.

Even when hormones worked, she was careful to add, they could only stall the disease's advance, not permanently stop it.

One hormone might stem the onslaught for a while—fourteen months, on average—before the tumors, growing resistant, would start to multiply and we'd have to try another. Eventually we'd run out of fresh reinforcements, and then it would be time for chemotherapy. At the sound of the word, I pulled in tighter. She continued briskly. But once the cancer had gone this far, chemo, too, was just a temporary blockade. The disease almost always broke through.

Except, maybe, there was one possible hope. A new treatment was showing promise in women whose cancers had gone this far. The therapy was called a bone marrow transplant, although it wasn't really a transplant, more an extreme form of chemotherapy. She took a breath. See, the problem with conventional chemo was it wasn't strong enough to destroy all the cancer cells once the disease had spread. No matter what kind you used, a few always survived. Researchers had found that in test tubes, however, high doses would wipe out all the cells. These doses had to be so high, though, that in real life, they'd kill the patient, too, by destroying her bone marrow, the fluid that contains the essential ingredients of the immune system. Then someone happened onto a solution. Remove a quantity of the bone marrow first, and you could reinject it—transplant it—after the bombings. This was called the "rescue." Immune system back in place, the patient would survive. Theoretically.

Transplants weren't without dangers, she had to let me know. Twenty percent of the patients died (a figure that's since dropped to 10). Other people never fully recovered. Their immune system couldn't get back up and running, or their hearing or kidneys were damaged for life. Permanent neuropathy, a numbness in the hands or feet, was often a problem. My heart, which had started to rise, sank again. She leaned back. But transplants were better than what they'd had before. And maybe 20 percent of patients achieved a worthwhile remission, a couple of years—with some, perhaps even a cure, though the technology hadn't been around long enough to say. The odds of this were tiny. But they were odds.

"There's hope. I just want you to know there's hope," Kruze said, whisking back the prospect as soon as she'd held it up. "Although you may have had too much radiation already to qualify for a transplant. I went to school with the guy who invented it. I'll call him tonight and find out."

"I'd like to do it," I said, still back on "hope." "As soon as possible. Maybe next month."

"Oh, no," she said. "You can't just show up and have a transplant. They require you to have months of chemo first, before you can begin. And you have to be accepted into the program. It takes a long time. We don't do them at the hospital. We'd have to find you a place that does."

She pushed my file back. Other patients were waiting.

"I'll see you in a few days," she said, rising. "If you have questions—"

"How long do I have?" I asked, not moving from the chair.

"The way this has come on so fast, it makes me think it's aggressive. If so, a year or two," she said.

And if not?

"Five. Maybe ten," she said with a matter-of-factness that I mistook at the time for efficiency.

"But don't worry," she said, gesturing toward the door. "We can keep you comfortable."

This cannot be, I thought in the elevator down. A year to live? A year? I feel fine. But wasn't that what the doomed patients all declared in the made-for-TV movies? I hadn't really seen one, Bonner's inadvertent challenge aside, but I could hear a bland, blond actress say these words, could imagine a roomful of drunken college freshmen playing the question at two A.M.: What would you do if a doctor had just told you you had only a year to live?

I would eat whatever the hell I wanted.

Fuck everything that moved on campus, man.

Rob a bank and go to Tahiti. What could they do to me? Send me to the chair?

No one would have gotten the answer right:

Walk out of the doctor's office, spend fifteen minutes trying to find a cab, and stride into the office before nine-thirty, purposefully appearing determined, so nobody could guess. It's far-fetched, paranoid, to think your assistant might wonder, Hmmm, my new boss looks upset—could that be because she's just found out she has terminal cancer? But it's far-fetched, at thirty-seven, to have been told that in the first place.

I spent the morning reading through manuscripts with a calm I later identified as shock. On automatic pilot, I kept a lunch date with a staff writer. She talked and I answered, and only once did I feel as if I'd left my body, when a thought pushed to the front of my mind: *She doesn't know it, but I'm dying.*

In the week that followed, I kept it up. Pulling against the tug of mania, I became resolutely practical. I tried to make death mundane by approaching it as a project. A window in my apartment had jammed. I canceled the appointment to have it fixed. Why spend the money? My estate could pay. Vocabulary had always been a passion, but now when I read, I no longer bothered to look up new words. What did it matter what *mirate* meant? I had all the words I needed. Where I was going, I wasn't going to need any more.

"Language is one of the things that makes us human," a shrink friend later said. "You were preparing to stop being human." Indeed, I was withdrawing. I also felt betrayed.

My whole life I'd loved language with a purity of devotion. Language was salvation. You could talk your way in and out of things, swim through streams of words into corners of truth. But at the oncologist's that morning, words had been damnation. "A year or two"—I'd never been so hurt. Language was not beauty now, it was foul.

In the slow-motion state I remembered from the first time I was sick, I worked hard, even when the new editor asked me to assign a piece on hypochondria. "You know?" she said. "Like the way everyone thinks they have brain tumors these days." I canceled plans for night, however, not wanting to have conversations. Alone in my apartment, I oscillated between moments of terror and contemplation. Mortality obliterates triviality; cut off from the easy worries of ordinary life (was that shirt at the cleaner? would the writer get his piece in on time? who the hell cared?), I was left with the exhausting big questions: If values were what you valued, what did I? I had no time for things I didn't cherish. Urgency was a lance. I could deflect it by using it to scratch out lists. What did I value? I wrote down traits. Loyalty, singularity, dependability, humility, courage, and optimism, although I was currently short on the last two.

Writers were next. Whom had I meant to read but hadn't? Milan Kundera was first. "Which of his books are you interested in?" the clerk in the bookstore clerk asked. The answer made me feel pathetic, but I said it. I was looking for *Immortality*.

Grief fragmented personality for a time. The inner machinery was busted up. Old lessons and phrases whirred in my head: *If you wanna win, you'd better be good.*

Good girl. Good as gold.

Made good. Good for you.

Good for you.

Good was the way. It's how you triumphed, right?, how you trumped a disease that was, literally, bad to the bone. Subdued by grief, I was inclined at first to become compliant, pleasing. In my grief, I forgot the reaction I'd had to the frail turbaned woman I'd encountered a month before, when meeting Claire for a lecture at Sloan Kettering Cancer Center. "Thank you, dear," the woman had said when I'd held the door for her. "Thank you so much. I'm still not strong enough." Her voice trembled in an excess of gratitude, triggering a flash of contempt in me. I would never let cancer make me docile like that, I'd thought at the time, but already, it was.

The docile, of course, are easy prey. One well-known study showed that it was the nastiest patients on the cancer floor, the sons of bitches, who did the best. No one ever got rid of cancer by being polite to it. In the long run, in fact, what would help me the most were the exact traits that got me kicked out of private school in eighth grade: surliness, fury in the face of disrespect (and what is cancer if not disrespectful? I had to take care not to be furious all the time), ill-tempered feistiness, a sneering disregard for authority that wasn't earned. Maybe that's because cancer behaves like a wilding adolescent. Healthy cells grow for a few months, then die off to make way for new ones. Cancerous ones refuse to accept limitations; they defy the body's signals and rules and run away from their home sites, hell-bent on living forever. Maybe, in order to fight it, you have to get down on its level, try to make yourself just as bad.

In the beginning, however, I was trying desperately to be good. I was good on the job, where no one knew, and didn't for months. After the reaction the last time, I was not about to tell. Stashing my resolve to apply temperance to my work, I volunteered for everything. I was an editor at the magazine, and most editors didn't write, but if a story needed an author, hey, I could do that. My workload quickly became staggering. In one assigning meeting, I was dismayed to find I was being tagged to write a piece on the "new waif models," who, as far as I could see, were absolute ringers for the old waif models. I was on the verge of exhaustive collapse, grappling with mortality, and I was supposed to report on supermodels? I imagined my editor's surprise when I turned in a piece that said, "Claudia may be out of favor, but she should at least be thankful she's not dead."

But supermodels, it turned out, were just the ticket, the perfect counter to the mordant thoughts that were obsessing me. In the course of my research, I developed an opposing obsession. "I have to tell you this," I'd inform puzzled friends who'd called to ask if there was any medical news. A few knew. Not many. "Linda might be doing *Victoria's Secret.*" Supermodels were performing the same function for me that celebrities provide for a lot of Americans. They diverted me from my life.

On good nights, they could even quiet the dirge in my head. Bad nights, it blared. "Death inhabits my bones, I can hear it cackling," I wrote floridly in my journal, scaring myself with the thought. "Stand porter at the door of thought," my father used to counsel us, and when his language turned Victorian like that, I knew he was quoting Mary Baker Eddy. Bad nights, the door was unguarded as I tried to imagine what the tumors looked like. Clots? Knots? Spurs? They were in there. I had to know. "Remarkable how hidden we are to ourselves," I wrote. "Doctors can see plainly into me, but I'm dense, inscrutable, to myself." My mind skimmed my body, again and again. No amount of guard-dogging was going to stop it, for in just one month, the pain I'd read about had begun.

One morning when I woke, I noticed a weird thrum coursing through my back, as if the bones had a metallic core that could channel electricity. When I felt it again a few nights later, at three A.M., I was beset by strong and immediate claustrophobia. *My body is dangerous*, I panicked, crying out to the bedroom walls, *I have to get out, oh, please, please.* As I begged the air, I realized with horror that no one could help me. Not my parents. Not doctors. Only, maybe, God.

But I'd stopped speaking to God.

Through repetition, the night terrors flayed me and I entered that state of extreme vulnerability that a friend describes as "skinless." Unarmored, I registered everything, too much. The day I started on Tamoxifen, the hormone, the paper reported two cancer deaths: Audrey Hepburn's, from colon cancer, and one of Jack Kevorkian's clients, of asphyxiation to avoid pain from cancerous tumors that had spread—my eyes widened—to his bones. The articles made my eyes sting with tears, but I couldn't stop myself. I read every word.

Unarmored—docile—I was an easy mark for the kind of bully whose breath quickens at hints of weakness.

At a CAT scan, the technician was a sadistic little man who took delight in disciplining me. "Move your arm to one o'clock. I *told* you, one o'clock." "Hold your arm up. I *said* hold your arm up." Before I'd gone in for the test, he'd given me four glasses of water. "Drink all of it," he ordered. "Your bladder has to be extended."

As the hour wore on, pressure built till I couldn't stand it. "Is this almost over?" I called out. "I really have to go to the bathroom." But the technician ignored me. He started and stopped the test, dragged it out. Finally there was nothing else he could do to delay. I was finished. Instead of freeing me, he picked up the phone. "Please," I shouted, "get me out." He glanced over and turned away. Frantic inside the machine, I tried to tear the needle out.

The tests came back. The cancer wasn't in my liver, or my lungs. But no doubt now, if I'd had one: It was in my bones. The thrum was a muezzin. Sharp pains soon followed, congregating along my spine. A rough-surfaced stone was growing in my coccyx, I learned one day when I lowered myself onto a bus seat and felt its quick jab. My God! It hurt to sit. A few days after, it hurt to lie. The mattress had grown too hard. Its pressure heated the bad spots along my back. If I lay on them too long the wrong way, the spots could begin to burn.

The worst pain was beneath my shoulder blade, where a rib throbbed so hard at times, I wanted to reach back and tear the bone out. "Have you called the doctor about it?" Claire asked. I had. I'd left messages with her receptionist a couple of times. But she wasn't calling back.

The second time I'd phoned to say, "Tell her this feels like a shotgun blast," the receptionist cut me off: "I know. Okay? I told her. All right?" By my third try, her snarl left no doubt: What she had here was a harassment caller. "Okay," she sighed. "Yeah. Okay." Soon, I was glad to get the office answering machine, which clicked on about half the time. "Something's come up and I have to reschedule my appointment. Please call," I'd tell it, confident that tape was the way to go. I was down on record. They had to phone back. But after a month of unanswered machine messages, I had to concede I was speaking into the void.

Sometimes, I did get through. "You're paying way too much attention to your body," Kruze scolded me after I called about spotting, from the Tamoxifen. "It's understandable, but you need to start thinking about other things."

Like what?, I wonder now. What would she have suggested a newly diagnosed terminal cancer patient think about: The Kentucky Derby? Warming trends in Africa? The Democrats' response to the Republican cooption of family values?

Bonner had never rebuked me for reporting a side effect. Kruze was fast making it clear that she was a very busy woman, and I was acting like one of those pettish old ladies who phones up doctors' offices for attention. I chafed at her brusqueness, but made a decision to try to win her over. If I could, I wouldn't have to consider that I'd left a perfectly good doctor for one whose profile was higher, but who was, increasingly, arrogant and indifferent.

On the next visit, I told her about the gun-blast pain, but didn't lodge a complaint about the unanswered calls. Too antagonistic. "That might be tumor flare," she said, referring to an odd property in which hormones sometimes initially increase pain before easing it. If tumor flare was what I had, it was a sign the Tamoxifen was working. "We'll have to wait and see. But if it doesn't improve, I want to send you for radiation."

She handed me a prescription for codeine. Visit over. I thought of questions I wanted to ask: Hadn't she said that radiation could disqualify me from a transplant? And wasn't the transplant my best hope? But questions made her impatient, made me unlikable. I'd figure out a plan on my own. I could sidle out of radiation, just not go. I could live with the pain for a while, if I had to. All things considered, it wasn't that bad.

Nights without sleep were prodding me to the edge. The codeine almost pushed me over. It was a relief, the way it first knocked me out when I took it at eleven, but the effect didn't last. By three, I was awake again, jittery from the dregs of the drug. Eventually I'd manage to fall back asleep, usually just before the alarm went off. All morning, I'd drink coffee to try and clear the codeine hangover.

Codeine wasn't the only chemical jangling my nerves. The Tamoxifen was producing nuclear winter–grade depression, wide hormonal mood swings that were magnified by exhaustion. All three, the fatigue and the two drugs, combined into a crying jag that lasted most of one weekend in February. Much of it is a blur to me now. "You have a choice," I remember rasping in the shower, but about what, I don't know. I also remember that a man I hardly knew but had confided in came by at one point and took me out for food. That night he called to see if I was all right and to tell me a funny story. Materializing at a crucial juncture, disappearing soon after, he was like an angel on the highway. His appearance was the first in a string of apparent miracles that were about to explode—not all at once but in short, wild bursts that, in retrospect, seem perfectly timed.

The first turning point came shortly after the lost weekend. If it's true that God works in mysterious ways, in this case, God went with a PBS special. While half-watching a show on the mind's effect on cancer, too zoned to pay close attention, I thought I heard a doctor say, "Patients who are happy do better."

I'm sure he didn't put it that flatly, but that's w
heard, and that's what I chose to believe.

I'm under medical orders, then, to be happy,

My new determined-happiness approach w
Screw you, cancer, you can take my body, but you can't take my mind.
It gave me control: If I had to go out, I could go out mewling, or
I could be remembered for the dignity and good cheer I'd shown.
Vanity made the call. I came down on the side of pluck.

"I'm putting myself under orders to be happy," I announced to
Ben, and he smiled broadly—*what a gal.* I'd thought he might.
I'd already figured out that people liked it when cancer patients
talked like this. Where I was still in the dark was regarding how
the hell I was supposed to put the plan into action.

I tried compiling a gratitude list, a technique I'd read about in
a magazine. At first it was a stretch: "I'm grateful I don't have
cancer in my liver. I'm grateful the pain isn't disabling. I'm grateful it looks like I can get insurance to pay for a bone marrow
transplant." I reread my efforts: Oh, yeah, this was certainly perk-
ing me up—my list was like a parody. But pressing on, I discovered I was grateful, besides, to have "a lot of good friends, and a
good job, and an apartment I like, and a family that's in good
shape." (I was still in my good phase.) My life wasn't a complete
mistake. Folding the paper, I put it in my wallet. From time to
time, I took it out and added to it.

The list was a start. Reading it would lift me for a while.
When I threatened to plummet, perspective took over. All perspective is the product of experience, and now that mine had
expanded to include a monthlong immersion in terror over death,
my views had widened. Before, I'd excelled at sulking over small
offenses. I could nurse a bad mood for days, but almost overnight, I lost the knack. As fear started to burn itself down—for
it's able to flame full-strength for only so long—I stopped having
to fake good cheer and became, at moments, genuinely cheerful.
Compared to the horror I'd been submerged in, most of my life

egan to look like a boon. I saw that I did, actually, have a choice. I could continue to let misery determine my life, or I could attempt to take pleasure in what blessings I found. That time, vanity didn't choose.

I don't mean to make it sound as if I became a blissed-out git. Terror still regularly swamped me. When that happened, the best I could do was run a checklist on myself: How am I right now?, I would make myself consider. Right now: Am I in a hospital? In a wheelchair? In unbearable pain? The answers, which I rediscovered thirty times a day if necessary, were, No, and No, and No. Right now, I was always pretty much okay, about the same as the previous fall when the pain had masqueraded as a bad back, the big difference being that, now that I knew, if I focused on the cause, I was terrified. Unchecked, terror bred terror.

In check, I was, perversely, more optimistic than I'd ever been. Not about my longevity, exactly. In my outlook. "Everyone's an expanding universe, and I am, too," I wrote one night. "There's no reason anymore to hold back. I want all the textures: silk, sandstone, the hair on a man's chest. I could live ten more years. I might even make fifty. I could love one more time. I could marry again. I could read a thousand books, swim in a mountain lake, learn forgiveness, embrace complexities. I could be given the time to grow. In love, and understanding."

In poleaxing me, the cancer had sent me sprawling back into darkness. But from the corner of my eye, I spied a small gleam of light, no more than a glowing scratch, the briefest flare of an afterimage. Turns out, I hadn't been wrong about language. I began exhorting myself out of the black airless place, singing in the language of light. I sang that gleam into a river, until its fast-rushing currents roared me down. I sang till I was stronger. And when I was ready, and when I could, I plunged in. And began kicking for my life.

BLIZZARD

THE RIVER RAGED AND, SOMETIMES, SO DID I. LIKE ALL prescriptions, my happiness plan had a few side effects. One was occasional intense annoyance.

"I'm sick of appreciating each day," I complained to Claire one morning after the effort had sent me to bed by nine. Acute awareness was driving me nuts.

"It's a pain in the butt to be up against your mortality every single minute," I said. "It's like having to remember to breathe. I don't want to smell one more freaking flower. I don't want the blueprints to be made constantly visible. I just want to be in a daze like everyone else, assuming I've got forever." I was walking around New York City full of unasked-for clarity, and the sudden wisdom was disconcerting. "It's like being on intravenous meditation," I said.

The river foamed and roiled, but it could be counted on to carry me. Except in the instances when I made the mistake of examining the current too closely, for then I saw what it was made of. Particles. That was it. I was being lifted up by particles, nothing more. And what were particles against the kind of darkness that had come into my life?

This kind of darkness was unrelenting. It was malevolent. It had let me know once, in January, that it intended to kill me. It delivered the message again on a gray Sunday in late February.

My spirits were good—the river was buoying me—but over the weekend, I became aware that my body was going into sudden decline. Something was progressing fast, but I couldn't tell what. The symptoms didn't seem oncological: Pinching pain in the back of my calf that was making me limp. Shortness of breath that had driven me off the StairMaster Sunday afternoon. By Sunday evening, continuous panting.

"Chills, fever, depression," Ben said, reading the Tamoxifen side effects from the *Physician's Desk Reference* over the phone.

"Vaginal discharge, vaginal bleeding, pulmonary embolism—Pulmonary embolism," he repeated. "Blood clot to the lung. Call your doctor."

Kruze was off duty. Another doctor admitted me to the emergency room, where I remained, a blood clot dissolving in my lung, on a gurney for four days.

"When are they going to move me into a room?" I'd ask Kruze on her visit each morning. Maybe later today, she'd say with an automatic smile, but my only official excursions out were for tests—pulmonary angiogram, blood gas measurements, scans, more scans. After the first night, I did make one lateral move, down a hallway and into the emergency ward. The size of a small pavilion, the room was bilious green and contained twenty cots, all occupied by patients in various stages of distress. One litter over, a young girl wearing two sweaters gagged yellow fluid into a pan. A man down the row looked fiery and gaunt. I hoped that what ailed him wasn't tubercular. A tuberculosis epidemic was on in New York City, the newspapers said, but only among the indigent, they hastened to assure readers. No one else had to worry—only people whose immune systems were impaired, by old age, say, or, well, some serious disease, like cancer.

Sliding under the covers, I tried to breathe through the sheets.

On the second day, I weakly attempted a rebellion. "I'm a journalist. I'm going to write about this," I tried threatening the weary-looking intern who'd come to examine me. He'd been in the middle of explaining that cancer, and not the hormone, might have caused the clot. Now he stopped and regarded me thoughtfully.

"You know, I wish you would," he said. "The hospital's been doing this for years. And be sure to mention that they charge people for a semiprivate room when they keep them here." Two cots over, a man groaned. The hospital had a point. No one could argue this was private.

Friends arrived at all hours with supplies. They'd wave a greeting to the security guard, who only enforced visiting times if you asked what they were. "This looks like the battlefield scene from *Gone With the Wind*," one said. Marshal law was in effect. To make a phone call, I had to sneak my IV pole past the guard and down a stretch of unheated hallway, into the main building. Once or twice, my calls were interrupted by two uniformed men who'd been dispatched to collect me. Mostly, no one noticed I was gone.

Army logic prevailed. Since the ward was set up to house emergencies, and since emergencies were by definition temporary, no one had thought to equip the place with showers. Even though some of the patients were logging real time, none of them were bathed. By the fourth day, when an orderly arrived to wheel me upstairs, my ankles were brown with dust; on the white sheets upstairs, my feet were gritty. After the thin cot in the ER, the mattress in the real semiprivate was a vast luxury— although a part of me felt, strangely, as if I'd been tamed.

I remained in captivity upstairs for two days. On the last morning, my family drove up to take me home. My father carried the one motley flower arrangement that had managed to track me down. I left with just the clothes I'd arrived in, plus a prescription for a new hormone, Meges. I didn't know yet that Meges was hated in cancer-support-group circles for its power to turn lean women into Big Gulps in a matter of months. "Fifteen pounds on average," Kruze warned when she came by with the prescription. "You're going to have to diet." She didn't buy her patients' line that they really weren't shoveling it in: "They don't know it, but they're eating more."

My caloric consumption hadn't changed much in twenty-four hours, when I saw my left arm had ballooned.

"This stuff is making my lymphodema worse," I reported to Kruze by phone from my home bed. My recent near-collapse had prompted a quick return call.

"What if I went back on the Tamoxifen?" I asked. "The doctor at the hospital wasn't sure it caused the clot."

"You're just going to have to tolerate the arm," she said. "The Tamoxifen wasn't working."

Not working? My stomach began to ache, as if I'd sucked down fetid gas.

"Your cancer has progressed significantly," she said. "They ran tests while you were in the hospital. The disease has advanced considerably. I'm very concerned."

There were a few sentences more, I think. I think she said she was no longer sure I was a candidate for hormone therapy. I believe she counseled me to try Meges anyway, on the grounds that a second hormone sometimes works when a first one fails. But by then there was too much stuffing in my head for me to hear. Hanging up, I glanced contemptuously at my left arm—in my life before, I'd actually consider its swelling a problem. Curling myself tight as a shell, I began to rock, whispering "very concerned" through tears until motion became punctuation and the phrase streamed into a wail.

Concerned . . . I wanted the bone marrow transplant . . . *Very concerned* . . . I didn't care how bad it was . . . *Concerned* . . . It was hope. I'd do it, do it now. . . .

I just wanted to live.

"What do you think you're going to do?" Claire asked that night. Along with the few friends I'd told, she'd taken to phoning daily. Their love circled me like bunting, helping keep me in one piece.

"Pray," I cracked. "But you know what? I can't even do that anymore. I don't want to talk to God."

"Do you think God wanted you to get sick?" she asked.

Actually, that *was* kind of what I'd been thinking, halfway, half consciously.

I didn't answer.

"Do you think God wants all those guys to die of AIDS?" she said.

Put like that, I saw the lunacy of this line of reasoning.

"No," I said. "No, I really don't."

"Look," she said. "Our bodies are vulnerable. We all get sick. We break down. It doesn't mean God is out to get us. It means we're human. We're not robots."

But sick like this?

Health sells in this culture, she said after a pause. Healthy hair, healthy teeth, healthy coats for our pets, and why do you think? Healthy revenues. Illness is invisible, we never see it reflected back at us, so it seems abnormal, or like a punishment. It's not, she continued; all illness is ordinary—unfortunate, in some instances, and hard, but ordinary. A hundred years ago, people knew that. They were regularly acquainted with suffering. Now it's different, she pointed out. Most people can, if only clumsily, evade suffering. Cancer patients can't. But suffering, along with joy, makes us human. If your mind remains open, she said, cancer can bring you to your own humanity.

I began praying again and, the morning after, woke to see white snowy ribbons unfurling from the roof across the street, a blizzard. It wasn't the first storm of the winter. But it was the first weather, of any kind, I'd noticed since the New Year.

My breathing improved. The rib pain got worse. I hoped this was extreme tumor flare. I saw Kruze, and I saw a pulmonary doctor, and I saw a Western herbalist, who sent me to a psychic healer.

I saw a Chinese herbalist, and an acupuncturist, and a social worker named Jean, and when I had time, I still saw Neden.

"It takes a village to raise a child," I told a friend, "but you need a tristate area to be sick."

Kruze increased my codeine level. I wasn't ready for radiation, I said. As she was filling out the prescription, I slipped in a question. "Do you still think I may only have a year?" I asked.

"A year?" she said.

"Remember, you said I might just have a year?" I tried again. "That if the cancer was aggressive, I, uh . . ."

Her pen hung in the air. She stared at me blankly.

"Um, remember, you said . . ." I began, then stopped. This made no sense. If you'd told someone she might only have a year or two to live, how could you possibly forget?

I tried another tack. "So. Then. I guess you think it might be more like five or ten, right?" I asked.

"Five or ten," she repeated distractedly, signing her name.

A week later, the pulmonary specialist was encouraging. "You're in good shape," he said, holding an X ray of my chest. He smiled shyly. I smiled, too. Boy, he could say that again. My latest round of tumor markers—the blood tests that measure cancer activity—had just come back. They were down by half. Meges was whomping the monster.

"You're fine," he said. "Except for the fractured rib, of course."

His smile stayed in place. Mine disappeared.

"Fractured rib?" I said. "What fractured rib?" But I knew exactly what rib. *The one that had been causing me pain on the order of a shotgun blast. The one my oncologist had failed to mention, or maybe even detect.*

"You mean she didn't tell you?" the pulmonary doctor said, clearly surprised, then caught himself and changed the subject. Had they drawn my blood yet, or did I need to see the nurse?

My composure held through the blood test. By the time I was in the elevator, my anger had turned to a viscose fear that was so thick, it made me sluggish. Once out of the building, I had to lean against a parked car. My back was to the sidewalk, so no one with a clear face could see I was crying.

In the cab, the rib began to ache. I shifted forward. The pain let up. I'd been pressing against the door. Hunching down beneath the driver's line of vision, I let the tears come. I was only now grasping just how mean cancer could be.

"Think you can fight me?" it had announced upstairs.

"Well, I can break your bones, easy.

"Anytime I want."

Crack.

Composure returned. The particles floated me. So did routine. At work everyone still regarded me as well. Some days I did, too. I was leading the life of a magazine editor: arm-wrestling agents over contracts, going to book parties, exploring the perks of the job.

"Going on one of those investigative facials?" my friend Judy smirked.

"Somebody has to," I said.

I was up for any investigative mission—undercover haircut, massage, chakra balancing, I'd do it—except on Tuesdays, when I'd begun to cut out early in order to make a five o'clock support group for Stage Four cancer patients. I'd been attending regularly since April, with mixed feelings.

"They're all so depressed," I'd said to Claire.

"I think that's understandable," she said.

It was, but I was a determined adherent to the screw-you-cancer happiness plan. We weren't always a good mix.

"This disease makes me feel so old," a woman my age said.

"What about the rest of you?" Jean, the social worker, asked. During the day, Jean worked at Sloan Kettering. At night she ran support groups.

"Actually," I said, "sometimes it makes me feel young."

"Why?" she said.

"Because whenever I tell someone, they say, 'But you're so young!' That's all I hear lately: 'You're so young!'"

One of the five women laughed. The others looked glumly at the rug. I made a note to myself to keep it wrapped. But if most of the group didn't share my skewed sense of levity, they were able to share in my concerns.

"I think you should tell your boss," one of them said. "I think she'll be okay. I've read her editor's letters. She seems human."

"But my last boss—" I said, then stopped. They'd heard the stories.

"I guarantee you, he was an anomaly," Jean said. "He must have been phobic about cancer. Most people just don't act like that."

"You should tell her," Jane, my favorite, said. "I think it would help you."

The sun was going down and the magazine halls were deserted when I stuck my head into my new boss's office. "Can I come in?" I asked, breathing fast. Not waiting for a response, I slid into a chair near her desk. Adrenaline and hyperventilation were making me faint. Alarm registered on her thin, tired face—I must have appeared slightly deranged—but I forged on and, in a rush, told her everything. She listened, and she nodded, and without missing a beat, she assured me she would help in whatever way she could. She said my job was secure. She spoke casually, as if she'd had dozens of conversations like this, just that year alone. The only time she betrayed surprise was when I asked her to treat me like the rest of the staff.

"I can keep up. I mean, I'm not sick," I said, forgetting to add, "in bed."

"Uh . . ." she said, blinking, then righted herself. "Okay."

"No one here has to know," I said. "The only thing they'll see is I'm going to get fat, from the treatment." The editor made a face, to show sympathy. She'd put on weight, she said, the year she'd started the magazine. I could borrow the large-size Chanels she'd had to buy. We laughed. The phone rang. She didn't answer it. The talk sputtered down into one about the annoyances of fat. The phone rang again, and she looked at it, so I thanked her and stood. Car headlamps were streaking Madison Avenue below when I walked out of her office, infinitely lighter, and into a designated safety zone.

I made an appointment with the radiation therapist. Her office was in the hospital basement, down the hall from the huge green machines. I had no intention of spending time in them in the near future; I would funnel codeine in a tube through my ear before I'd ruin my chance for the transplant. I was curious to see what she'd say.

Her remarks did not amount to a pep talk.

"You have lesions in your skull," she said, examining a lab report from my chart. "Do you have headaches? Memory loss?"

No, I did not. My tone was the one children use who've been accused of jumping on the bed when they've actually spilled Coke on the rug.

And: Weight loss? Had my pain increased? Could I show her where it was?

Concluding the list of degenerative symptoms, she turned to the X ray on the light box behind her. "A good portion of the bone has been destroyed," she said. Radiation could not fix that. What it could do was shrink the tumors, but only for a while. Eventually they'd probably return, then radiation might be useless. In general, an area could be radiated only once.

"We can begin next week," she said. "My secretary will set up the appointment."

"Sorry," I said, lifting my purse. "I've decided to wait. Why don't I call you when I'm ready?" I was even more adamant about holding out. If radiation was a one-shot defense, I wasn't going to waste it till I was desperate.

As the days wore on, my friends became adept at offering consolation. Practice made them limber. "I was talking to a woman who knew a woman who was on Meges," Claire would call to say. "Said she was on it for years."

"You're going to wipe the floor with that cancer," Ben said when I told him my tumor markers had dropped. "That cancer better be afraid. That cancer is toast."

"God doesn't give us more than we can handle," a new friend, Anna, ventured, and I refrained from rolling my eyes. She hadn't known me that long, so she was still a neophyte at this. Anyway, old saw, fresh insight—I didn't care. If it contained a sliver of hope, I'd take it.

I didn't say anything to Anna, but twice in the following month, God did.

The first episode was minor. A tailor laughed at me.

I'd come into her shop with piles of clothes that needed to be let out. Everything I owned was too small. Meges had put fourteen pounds on me in six weeks, even though, as I swore to Kruze, I'd been fanatic about counting fat and keeping up at the gym. "You're going to have to try harder," she said. "I've seen women gain forty pounds on this. If you do, we'll have to take you off."

At one size larger, I'd been a good sport. I bought jeans in a bigger eleven, a new skirt in a twelve. But when the skirt's buttons began to pull just three weeks later, I was despondent. This weight, which I could not keep down, represented the way my life was being wrest from my control. An unseen force was making me ill, making me fat. Making me miserable.

"Wow! That's tight!" the tailor hooted when I emerged from the curtain in a strapless black velvet dress that had skimmed me precisely the year before. When I'd worn it to a black-tie dinner with Ben, men's heads had turned. Now I was the one turning my head, away from the mirror. The woman in front of me was thick-waisted and dowdy. She had no business putting on a dress like that.

"I don't even know if there's enough material," the tailor said, and I kept my head up while she tugged, stood straight, no expression. I was perfectly disaffected. Till I got home.

"How *dare* it!" I raged, and "it" was the tailor who clucked; the drug that bloated me up ("like a waterlogged pig," I cried); the sorry ego that couldn't take a fourteen-pound knock. It was the cancer that was eating my bones, that throbbed in my back now, most mornings when I woke, like bongos. It was everything.

In the second episode, I returned home from the office and almost tripped on my cat, who was lying across the doorsill to the bedroom. "Butler," I called, but he only raised his head. It was clear he couldn't get up.

"I saw him eating one of my Meges. It's a hormone pill," I told the vet as we both stared down at the listless cat.

"That may be what's wrong," the vet said solemnly.

("The only thing Meges would have done would have been lower his voice," a doctor scoffed when I finally got up my nerve to ask about it. For years, I'd been convinced I'd accidentally poisoned my own pet.)

"Don't identify with the cat," Jean, the social worker, said after the cat had died, when I complained I couldn't eat, couldn't sleep, couldn't help but think: The vet had tried everything. Nothing, not medication, not an operation, could do any good, and didn't that have a familiar ring?

"Yeah," Diego said when I repeated her advice. "Don't identify. You do not lie under the bed and eat pills off the floor." Not normally, no. But I did lie on the bed, and for fifteen years, the cat had, too, curled beside me on the pillow. His fur and smell had been comfort. At a time when I needed it most, it was gone. The gunman was no longer in the building. He was up in the tower, a sniper now. As my life compressed down, got more narrow, he could fit the whole thing in his sight.

There was another episode, a third blow, too. This one didn't push me around the bend, though. It knocked me in the right direction.

At work my phone rang, and Claire demanded, "*What* is going on with you?"

"What?" I asked.

"I've just come from Kruze's," she said. "She's very worried by your behavior. She says you're not taking this disease seriously. She says you don't show up for appointments, that you're endangering your health."

"Not showing up?" I said, confused, thinking, She was talking about me with another patient—isn't that illegal? Not showing up? I was there all the time. Then I realized—all those times I'd tried to reschedule. All those messages that went unreturned. The days when I'd canceled, the receptionist must have neglected to remove my name from the patient list. Had Kruze seen it there, she'd have assumed I was blowing off appointments. I could understand why she'd been worried. But why hadn't she talked to me directly?

When I dialed her number, anger charged my voice so that, for once, the receptionist was meek. I got through right away.

"Is there a problem?" Kruze asked.

"I cannot believe you were discussing my case with another patient," I began slowly, before anger rushed me and I reeled off my complaints: I could never get her on the phone, her receptionist did not respond to my calls, she didn't respond to my questions, the receptionist was rude. I paused. She drew a sharp breath.

"We have hundreds of patients come through this office," she said, precisely enunciating each word. "We've never had a complaint before. I think the problem here lies with the patient."

But I didn't have a problem keeping appointments, I replied. I held a responsible job and—

"We've received letters from other doctors about you," she said. "You're not good with follow-up."

Letters? Who'd been writing letters?

"This is a difficult, mysterious case and you need to be followed closely," she said, sidestepping. "I do not think you are able to tell when you're in pain."

Yes, I'd said I had a high tolerance for pain, but if she'd been concerned by my ability to gauge it, why hadn't she called back all the times when I'd phoned about that pain?

"What times?" she said.

The times with the fractured rib—the rib that had been found by the pulmonary doctor, I couldn't refrain from adding, and not her. Look, I said. I need an oncologist I can talk to.

"That's it!" she said. "Your last sentence convinced me. I can no longer be your oncologist. I will give you the name of someone you can go to, but I am removing myself from this case."

And she fired me. After five months, and with a month to go before the determining scan, she fired me, leaving me with cancer that was creeping through my spine and, for the moment, no doctor.

"Wait," I said. I was sick, an advanced case, she'd said so. I had to be with a doctor. She couldn't. "The scan . . . I didn't mean . . . Can't we fix this?"

"I'm sorry," she said. "I think it's better this way." And when I found no compassion in her voice, just a wall, I was abject with despondence. I was so bad—so hopeless—even a woman paid to care didn't want me.

"Lawsuit," Ben speculated. "When you mentioned what happened with the fractured rib, she realized she was guilty of negligence. She took herself off your case because she was worried you were going to sue her."

"Difficult and mysterious?" Jean said when I called and wailed, "She doesn't want to treat me because she knows I'm going to die."

"From what you've told me," she said, "you've got garden-variety metastasized breast cancer. You're seriously ill, but you're not even in the serious end of seriously ill. She was building a case against you. For whatever reason, she decided you were a bad patient. You'd have spent all your time trying to prove you weren't. It's better to look elsewhere."

I did. I interviewed an oncologist who resembled Jack Klugman. He wanted to put me on chemotherapy for the rest of my life. He'd come up with a particular way of mixing drugs that had made him a name for himself—twenty years before, I found out after. I didn't know that all-chemo, all-the-time was his forte when I ventured, "But Meges is working. Why can't I stay on that?"

"Want to know how long that hormone will work?" he bellowed. "I'll tell you how long that hormone will work! Two to four months!"

I interviewed another who slumped in his chair and sighed as he told me I was not a good candidate for a transplant. "Cancer in the bone?" he said, shaking his head. "It's probably in your marrow by now. They'd just be retransplanting you with cancer." The rest of his answers were dispirited, too. A depressed oncologist—just what I needed. Remembering that the Indonesians believe depression is catching, I decided not to risk contracting a case.

I phoned two other prospects, both of whom came highly recommended. Neither was taking on new patients. A week went by, then a second. I was in a state of dread, perpetually vigilant for signs of danger, a turn. Having run out of leads for oncologists, I looked up the one my now-ex-doctor had suggested. Dr. F's qualifications were strong. His manner was impersonal, but he wasn't arrogant. He didn't want to switch my treatment; he'd keep me on the hormone another month, then order the scan. He was with the same hospital my records were. I wouldn't have to transfer. I signed on.

I wrote a letter of complaint to Kruze's department head. A month later, I received a copy of Kruze's response. "Miss Rich was admitted to the hospital with a pulmonary embolism and a full evaluation of her current problem was performed," she wrote. "It was determined at that time that there was no progression of her disease." No progression! Why had she told me, when I'd phoned about the lymphodema arm just after my release, that my cancer had advanced significantly, that she was "very concerned"? I thought of the despair she'd plunged me into—for no good reason, it appeared now, from her account. But had she lied to me then? And if so, why—to get me to stay on Meges? Or was she forgetting she'd said my cancer was raging, the way she hadn't remembered telling me I only had a few years to live?

"I can understand the pain and anger Miss Rich feels," the last line read, "but it is misdirected." Condescension didn't blur her meaning. She was claiming that because I had cancer, I wasn't able to perceive the facts. She was trying to use my illness to discredit me.

Two months after receiving the letter, I got a call from Claire. "Did you hear?" she said breathlessly.

Kruze was leaving medicine.

"She's shutting down her office," Claire said. "Sending everyone to other doctors. She said she's decided to stay home and spend more time with her children."

As I write, it's been six years. She's still with her children, as far as I know. Or at least, she's never returned.

In those flat weeks, while I looked for a doctor, I remained buoyant. Particles weren't what was carrying me, though. I'd nearly forgotten about particles by then. There was a force that was lifting me higher, but it wasn't the river and it wasn't routine.

I was giddy.

Just fine.

You know, life was a wonder.

Because in late spring, I'd fallen in love.

BOLT

AFTER THAT FIRST NIGHT OF COMPRESSED DESIRE, WHEN he'd turned to me in the blue-gray light of the video we'd rented and said, "This may be a mistake, but I'd really like to hug you," after he left my apartment at four A.M., then phoned midmorning the next day to ask, "Did I leave my belt there?" with such an obvious purr of happiness that I was reduced to embarrassed mumbling, right exactly after that, I closed my office door, phoned the shrink, and relayed what had happened, declaring, as melodramatically as whispering would allow, "I can't believe it. I wish he would die."

No you don't, Neden replied. I could tell he was as surprised as I. But professional training prevented him from indulging in the pleasures of double-speak hyperbole.

"All right, not die," I said. "Move to China. Not call again."

What's the matter? Neden asked. He'd thought I liked Ben.

I did. I adored Ben. In the last couple of months, Ben had been tenacious about investigating metastatic breast cancer on my behalf. He hounded the disease as best he could, and best for him meant research. He was a journalist. Information, as he saw it, was my strongest defense.

"Package here for you," the receptionist would unexpectedly phone back to say every so often. I'd come out to find another gray envelope thick with clippings, some from obscure medical journals. I preferred these, the articles with the tangled footnotes that Ben had cryptically circled. It was reassuring to stumble on sentences like "Identification and purification of the 'stem cell' responsible for repopulation of marrow and for sustained hematopoietic cell renewal have long been a goal of experimental hematologists." Scientists were clearly moving on the problem, though I couldn't always tell where. I hated the stories torn from popular newsstand magazines. In the quiet of my office, words like *dismal* and *two-year survival* would jump off the page at me like barking dogs.

Since I'd become sick, Ben had shown a deep, fraternal concern. I'd begun to regard him as a brother, and that was half the trouble. The other half was, I just didn't get it.

"It's like he's making fun of me," I was trying to explain on the phone. "I don't understand. What would make him want to get involved with me now?"

Why don't you ask him? the shrink proposed.

"I was going to bring it up if you hadn't," Ben said at the restaurant that night, shooting a quick glance up from his tureen of mussels. An intolerable shyness had overcome us both. To surrounding tables, we must have appeared to be two people speaking into our plates.

"Courage," he said somberly, addressing a green fleck in the broth. "Courage is a real turn-on. I was really turned on by how courageous you've been. And beauty. Courage and beauty. I've always liked you and thought you were attractive, but since you've gone to the magazine, you've really looked good."

By the time the waiter set down the Belgian-chocolate mousse, we were sitting up straighter, as if there'd been a shift of air pressure in the room. I examined his face as we discussed how to proceed, agreed to go slow. The slight pulsing light coming off his skin had no discernible source. Ben was beaming.

Outside my apartment building, before we went upstairs, he paused and held me. "I wish time would stop," he said.

Later he said, "You're like that dessert. Wicked. And sweet."

Ben left town. He had an assignment, in Detroit. When the weekend came, I went to a party. I went to the gym, I cleaned the apartment. I was floating.

On Monday night I'm floating once more, but in a different way. In bed I keep my eyes fixed on a painting of palm trees. The pain has gotten bad again. I've taken two pills tonight, the doctor said I could, and I'm skimming on reverie through the lush, ocher air of a codeine haze.

In these tropics, in my bedroom, I'm cresting on emotion, so smooth. I nurse languor with each breath. It's sweet, sweet like the way, I admit now, groggy and grinning, that I've loved Ben from the beginning. I let the thought "I love him now" skitter through my head as I mumble to the palm trees about how I don't want a savior, I just want him, I love to touch him, stroke his back, his hands. We're cruising together, Ben and I, and I love it, I love it, till I foolishly allow myself to replay the nights with him in my mind, and the ocher takes on the dirty yellow tinge of fear. The nights were too good. When I see him again, he could say they were a mistake, he's sorry, he can't, and I'm crashing. I don't want them to have been one flash of dreamlight in the long black stretch of these terrible months. The codeine tumbles me and I hit hard, because, of course, I'm not just worried that Ben will reconsider. I'm so afraid that I'll get sicker, and this will all end.

When Ben returns, he doesn't say anything like "My mistake." For the first three hours, he doesn't say much. We're at his apartment, a bachelor house. His blue couch is soft, except in the spots where his cat has shredded it and he's placed Scotch tape over the tears. We lie down, and when he touches me, the pain eases. I'm happy.

Later he tells me about a woman he loved, someone who treated him badly. "It was ten years ago," he says. "You'd think—ten years—but it's still painful. We were really in love. And the thing is, I could have the same feelings for you."

She left him, he said. And he's worried he'll leave me, that he won't be able to take it. We're in bed now, side by side, staring at a groining of light that's forming on the ceiling. He doesn't see me when I nod.

I do, I nod, because, for one thing, I'm not surprised. This guy was my friend for years. I already gathered he wrote the manifesto for men who can't commit. It's not a screed that's alien to me; I've contributed a few tracts on the subject myself. I nod because cancer and codeine's making me reckless, bold—so what, I'll take the risk. But mostly, I'm nodding acceptance. Once it's been stated, I see the worst isn't that bad. I can't tell if Ben can be strong enough. But I do know I loved him once without hope that he'd love me in return, and that had to have been harder than any bad ending that might happen.

Shadows are vaulting the ceiling. I reach over and trail a finger over his cheekbone. He shifts his head, smiles. I smile back. Since I never thought I'd have him, all this is gravy. If he left me, it would be awful. But if he did, I'd survive.

Two dreams wake me the first week in June. Neither requires the services of Dr. Jung. In one I've gone to Switzerland. I'm trying to buy a watch, but the man will only sell me a small one. A watch, get it? Time. In another, Lynn appears. We're straddling a bench, facing each other, playing cards. Another winking nudge from the subconcious, a dream for the remedial sleeper. Because what Lynn and I are playing for is, of course, time.

On the afternoon of the first whole night we plan to spend together, I stop into a small lingerie shop on my way back from the gym. My top drawer needs replenishing. Nothing in it fits anymore. Behind the curtain, I'm wrestling with a strap when I hear a gruff, familiar voice. "Do you still have that sleep shirt I was asking about a few days ago?" Ben. "Ben!" I cry, grabbing the curtain and circling out so the fabric wraps around me like a sarong. Caught in the middle of examining undies, he looks grimly shocked. Then he breaks into a grin.

"Do you two know each other?" the salesgirl asks as we both laugh and one of us squeals.

"Yes, we—" he says.

"Have plans for tonight," I inform her.

"*Uh*-uh! I don't believe it," the salesgirl exclaims, and we all three shake our heads.

That was like an O. Henry story, he and I agree as we emerge from the store carrying bags packed with tissue.

The sleep shirt is thick silk, a cream stripe imprinted on cream. "It's beautiful," I whisper when he formally presents it that evening. I quickly slip it on—then hug my body so he can't see it's way too tight. The sleep shirt's a medium. I've become a true large. Ben doesn't indicate he's noticed, but he must have. When later he says, "You're so sexy. Men must flock to you," I check him for signs of veiled sarcasm or pity, but his brown eyes are narrowed. He's serious. I'm fatter than I've ever been, bloated from cancer treatments, and he thinks men are flocking to me. Well, one is. The one I want.

Some things I do with Ben that I haven't done before: Sit willingly for sweeping romantic gestures (he brought a book of ancient Chinese poetry to a coffeehouse, for instance, and read it to me out loud) and don't think, Boy, is this embarrassing. Make out in the back row of a movie theater. Fool around in the back of a cab. Learn the steep and intricate pleasures of a foot massage.

Swoon in an eighth-grade manner about the boy to the members of the support group.

I'd lead with an oncological concern, then catch a quick dog-leg. "I didn't need to have the X ray, after all," I said, "but since I'd left work anyway, I went to Ben's. He's so cute." The tactic wasn't really washing. I had an idea I was becoming the most unpopular person in the group. One woman in particular, Nancy, was shooting me daggers. "You just don't know yet how bad it is," she'd hissed when we were alone together in the elevator.

I couldn't help it. I was a goner. Besides, if these women wanted to talk alternative healing, I had a few suggestions. I hadn't realized how angry I'd been with my body—damn lump, damn scars, damn splintering, collapsing bones—until I lay on the couch with Ben and he kneaded me, lightly at first, then fast and deep, till *soma* welled and flowed over me, washing the anger away. Little by little, he was returning my body to me.

One thing I don't do: talk much about the pain. Some days now, it's so strong I take short, slow steps so no one will know about the rusting bolt that's pushing deeper into my hip. If I walk fast, at a subway rate, the bolt scrapes and hurts and makes me bite my lip. I hide this from Ben, play it down, because I don't want cancer to sour one minute with him. He's busy; the amount of time we can get together is limited. I want all of it to be good.

Ben's work keeps him sequestered for days. He's got magazine stories to do, and he's signed to write a book. He has to concentrate. We're settling into a pattern: We get together once or twice a week, usually times and places he decides. I don't like it. With the passion of the converted, I hate work obsession. Besides, I don't like being alone right now. But I'd race in front of him across

Grand Central before I'd say that. I will not appear needy. Bad enough that my illness makes such exorbitant demands.

Alone, I ward off thoughts like, *Cancer has become like a deadly sporting event. It's all in the pacing now. I have to get through each day. I have to get through the next three weeks.* The deciding scan is less than a month off.

On lucky days, when the bolt feels slick and allows me to sit without wincing, I can still convince myself that the world will continue to widen out, that the sun will always streak the East River, that the morning pavement will forever be hard and important and cool, and the early-summer afternoon heat will settle men onto the benches of Union Square Park to appraise the pigeons and girls. On days like this, all it takes is a run through the gratitude points, which I'm continually revising and reshuffling. "... that I'm living now, when there's more treatment than ever available; that I'm learning to love a man again; that I'm able to take joy in the clear, warm weather ..."

But even on the unlucky days, when I have to press on the hip to keep it from throbbing, when I lie in bed and breathe the soft night air of June and wonder, with a sharp pang, if this might be my last summer, even then there are moments when I think, But I've never been so happy. On those days, I'm shielded by one of the inverse properties of serious illness. When its stay is extended, I'm learning, cancer demands that you rejoice in life. Your soul multiplies against the invading cells—for every action there's a metaphysical reaction—you invoke pleasure to offset the pain.

When the bolt twists too deep and my leg begins to drag, so lightly I can't be sure I'm not imagining it, I call Dr. F, who orders X rays to rule out fractures. "But I don't think this could be a fracture," I say, baffled; nothing stings, as it would with a broken bone. After a while, I'll figure it out: If I call with a complaint, F will send me for a test, every single time, automatic. Lawsuit medicine, I begin to think of this approach. I've been a recipient before, but not on this order. Everyone in F's practice seems to subscribe to it. Once, a covering colleague tells me not to use the StairMaster because I could fall off.

"You've got a lot of lesions here," he says. "I don't want you calling me in the middle of the night with a fracture."

"Anyone who falls off a StairMaster should call a neurologist, not an oncologist," I answer, unwilling to forgo the painkilling endorphins the exercise produces, but with lawsuit medicine, common sense isn't the point. Malpractice avoidance is. The colleague's warning, like half of F's tests, remind me of those stickers on ladders that state the hazards of climbing them—unnecessary, except to the lawyers.

I'm not surprised when the X rays show nothing, relieved when the leg improves on its own.

Ben has to go out of town again. In Miami a wild-man famous novelist has a book coming out. Ben's been assigned to profile him. By the time he calls from his hotel room, I'm swelling on longing and codeine and the candle-glow sight of a pale full moon crowning a building down the street. Do you miss me? he asks from the actual tropics. Yeah, I say softly, gliding on his voice into reflections about moons over Miami and Manhattan and ". . . nude cream-corn wrestling," he says, chuckling. "The guy hangs out at a bar in the Keys that has it. Tomorrow I want to pick up my old friend Cindy and see if I can find it, put it in the piece. Do you believe this guy? I've heard of Jell-O, but creamed corn?!"

"I certainly do hope you have fun tomorrow, with your friend," I say, but I'm not really jealous of the woman—though it wouldn't be so bad if Cindy slipped into a vat and choked to death on corn. I want to be on the road, searching for the right seedy bar, on an adventure of my own in the Keys.

Two weekends before the scan, Ben's back, but I have to leave town. My friends Daniel and Nicole are getting married, in

Bucks County, Pennsylvania. Outdoors, behind the house her father built, flanked by two pots of lilacs, they stand before a fat minister named Mabel, who clears her throat and begins. "We're here to be blessed by this union . . ." No one coughs or sways much during the ceremony. The couple are gentle and eager to be married, nothing hidden or blackened about them. A conviction hangs in the air that this is one that can last. Shrieks do, too; two boys in short pants chase each other through the crowd, but no one seems to mind.

Nicole and Daniel say they do. The crowd trickles forward, then surrounds them like a wave. I retreat, pull a chair to the edge of the patio, too exhausted from the drive to stand for long on the grass. It's just me here, and the caterers. Ben is about to start reviewing his interview notes. He thought he'd better not come.

Squinting into the sun, I can see Daniel, a jocular guy, clamp an arm around a buddy. Nicole's first husband was taciturn, she told me, he almost never spoke. If opposites are the key, I consider, I'm nowhere near a lock. Diego: journalist who lives for his work. Ben: journalist who'd kill for his. Obviously, my brief immersion in the lessor's self-help books didn't take. I've been impervious to the warning about going out with "the same man, different face," unheeding of the advice to "become the person you want to be, not date him." Maybe I'm just a woman who can't love enough, or wisely, because addled as I am over Ben, in the throes of lust and love, I can't imagine the two of us ever staking our place between the lilacs.

"Nothing scares me much anymore except, funnily enough, marriage," I write at home that night. "Last time, it made me harden and shrink. It sapped my life. Now I'd be loath to burden someone else with my cancer, to bring them into the terrible daily reality of it. Cancer will eventually destroy my body. How can I allow anyone I love to watch the long, drawn-out, painful deterioration up close? How can I be married again? I'm afraid the destruction would destroy their love."

"But I am not my cancer," I reverse myself two paragraphs on, a little bored with this noble vision of myself sparing some nameless man (Ben) my messy and interminable demise. "I've got many balancing assets: spirit, and intelligence, compassion, good humor, optimism, strength." I'm so busy retallying my many fine traits that I overlook one point: Ben can barely be persuaded to leave his apartment more than once a week as it is, and he's showing no inclination toward stepping up the frequency. It doesn't appear likely I'll have to hold him at arm's length. He already is.

Over lunch with the writer for the hypochondria piece, the talk turns to the medicalization of America, the way even criminal behavior is being respun as illness ("shoplifting is a disease").

"What do you think about Breast Cancer Awareness Month?" I ask, not mentioning I've developed some awareness on my own. Leading her, I add, "Isn't there a way it makes the illness into spectacle?"

"Yeah, I'm sick of those pink ribbons," she says. "The number-one killer in the world is dysentery, but you don't see anyone going around wearing brown ribbons, do you? It puts me off, how ribbons romanticize illness."

"Right. Breast cancer's just another disease," I say, with more emphasis than an editor might give to a story discussion. "Come on; it's just a fucking disease."

The weekend before the scan, Ben has to leave town again, for an interview in Washington, but this time I go with him. Saturday noon, his work concluded, we rent a car and drive into the Virginia countryside, to Leesburg and my mother's family home, Rock Spring, where my aunt now lives. White and columned, with a fireplace in each bedroom, Rock Spring was the capital of the United States for a night, when the British burned Washington and Dolly Madison, fleeing, stayed there. Or so my mother maintains. "Wherever the state papers are, that's the capital," she says. "She brought the papers with her, so we were the capital of the United States." We'll get in a fight if I mention that another grand old home in the area makes the same claim. Fine; Dolly Madison slept around.

At Rock Spring I'm giddy, flashing back to my childhood summers, recalling diving under a blanket one night as my sister shrieked, "I saw the ghost! He's in the fireplace!" That afternoon I'd said, "During the war, they hung a Yankee in the dining room. It's true. Mom told me." Under covers in the bedroom, we realized our plight. Technically we were Yankee children. He had come back to claim his own.

My aunt doesn't put us in the ghost's room, but in the bedroom where, once, as my great-grandmother lay sleeping, my cousin Rick and I snuck in and released a jar of fireflies. An hour later, our sides still hurt from laughing at the thought of her face, till one of us said, "What if she gets a heart attack?," and we couldn't sleep all night. When we crept downstairs the next morning, she was at the table eating sausages, still alive. At breakfast we studied her carefully, but if she had any inkling she'd escaped death by flashing light, she didn't give a sign.

On Saturday night Ben and I join my aunt and uncle on the porch for crabs. Sunday morning we go for a drive. It's a wonderful weekend, except for the moment when, contemplating how much I love Rock Spring, I think, This may be the last time I'm ever going to see it. But by now I've had this same realization about 150 other times, about 150 other things. In some cases, I've already had second sightings. The drama is wearing thin. I make myself ignore the thought, just as I've ignored the pain that's beat steadily in my back the whole weekend.

On the plane I'm still giddy till I press against Ben and sense him stiffen. Just slightly, but enough that I pull back and smooth my jeans, which, of course, have no wrinkles. For the rest of the flight, we read.

In the cab he barks out addresses to the driver, his first, then mine, as if it's just assumed that we'll go our separate ways. "Ben, can't we . . ." I start to say—pain's licking my back, the scan's Tuesday, I don't want go home alone—but he turns his face sharply toward me, takes a deep breath, sighs.

"—tell him we want the bridge?" I finish quietly. The shade of annoyance that had crossed his face vanishes. My frustration doesn't. I've never had so little control in a relationship, just as, no coincidence, I'm sure, I've never had so little over my body. For now I say nothing. I don't want the shade to grow into a blackness that swallows Ben up so he disappears.

Thursday. My father's birthday will be on Thursday this year. And my mother's will be on Monday, and the wheat-colored disk of the bone scan machine has only moved another milli-jot toward my feet, and if I have to calculate one more birthday, I'll go full-rotting blown-out insane. *Hold your breath*, the mechanical man says. *Now breathe*. He says it, *breeeeathe*, like "breeze," swingy, with a hint of fun. *Breeeeathe*, the machine is recording my future as it clicks and whirs. *Breeeeathe*, the man is implacable, he can't be bribed or persuaded. Nothing I think or do now will in any way change the picture. *Thy will, not mine, be done*, I pray to God, since it just dawned on me that's what's going to happen anyway, might as well ask for it, get points. *Thank you in advance, please just give me the grace and strength to handle it, whatever the results may be*, I continue, and the scanner murmurs some machine-dream answer as it nudges the disk along.

NOTHING. Nothing! Nothing. *Nothing*. The scans are back and they're showing nothing, no new bone cankers, only the same dits from before, the best results we could have hoped for. Nothing from something is everything: no progression.

I knew it: The Meges is working, it's holding the line. I knew it the other day, when a surge of energy propelled me out of bed, when I bent, effortlessly, to pick up a shirt, when I walked to work so briskly—triumphantly, I can see now.

"I knew it," I tell Claire, and she screams. So did she!

"I knew it," I tell Ben, who gives a roar of delight and promptly calls me Robobabe. "That's what you are," he says. "You're a Robobabe."

I knew, know it, right up till the moment when the phone rings and his secretary puts Dr. F on the line. F has to talk to me about the tumor markers. The blood tests. I forgot.

"The lab must have screwed up," he says. "The markers are 252, up from 99 in April. I'm going to ask them to run them again. These numbers don't make any sense. I'm sure they're a mistake. That happens. If you hurry, you can get in before they close." It's Friday, three o'clock; we're wobbling on the edge of the long July Fourth weekend.

Racing, I make it to the lab and get myself tapped again. Like sap, I think, spirits holding, but by Saturday morning, they're sputtering down into free fall. By Saturday night, I'm chattering with dread. Has the cancer invaded another organ? Is that why the numbers are up? Sunday I wake from a vague dream about Lynn. The details are hazy, but the last scene is pointed: I'm going somewhere, to join her.

The weekend ticks by, each second a small lash, and when on Tuesday the report still isn't back, the seconds bite deeper. Wednesday morning, as I wait for F's office to open, they don't just cut anymore, they slash.

At ten I call. Yes, the secretary says. Just a minute, the markers came in. Hold on, she'll find them, and as I wait, I don't feel the long sleepless hours, just calm. On hold, I'm the miraculous possessor of infinite serenity, because suddenly I know

173

again. I know. The news will be good. I know, because it has to be.

Okay, the secretary says. They're right here. Just one second more. She has to open them.

And that second's anesthesia, but the next one's raw.

Three twelve, the secretary says, does that sound right?

312.

No mistake.

There's a problem.

CURL

FOR THE REST OF THE SUMMER, THE DANGER REMAINS unnamed. For the summer, and into the fall. The danger is coming, but it's wily. It won't show itself directly. The danger is a master at dalliance, at savoring the suspense. For now it crouches off in the distance, taunting us through tumor markers.

"Doctors don't like to go on markers alone," the social worker Jean says, "because markers can be unreliable. Something like a cold can throw them off. Some places won't even use them." I've noticed that the lab always prints a disclaimer on the tests: "For investigational purposes only. Not to be used for diagnostic purposes without confirmation by another procedure." But obviously they're not being used for entertainment purposes either, or why would so many oncologists run them? For every deadbeat of a marker, there must be two, at least, that read right, and my rising pain makes me think my rising numbers are prophetic.

Still, the only solid piece of business F has is the scan, and the scan is showing nothing, so that's what we do. "I have to know what I'm treating," he says. "I don't see anything new here to treat.

"It may be time to start talking about chemotherapy," he cautions. "I'm not saying it's time for chemotherapy. But it may be time to start talking."

Soon he'll need to hand me the nuclear-explosion device. The warning dreams have taken form, come to life. No metaphorical night goblins now; I really am playing for time.

The end of summer deals me a surprise: a straight flush of idyllic weekends, the kind that spin out so shimmering and smooth, you don't realize till later that, at moments, you were reeling on just the sweetness of the light. I'm happy in the Hamptons, standing on a lobster restaurant's curl of a beach, as Ben holds me and rocks me and hums tunelessly while we watch the sun melt into the sea. Happy in Boston, on a visit with an obsessed filmmaker, who shows us the rushes on his new find, an incurious, worn-out lion tamer. In Connecticut, at a party on a film actor's estate, when we hold hands in wicker chairs in a field and describe faces in the clouds. Even on a trip to see Ben's mother, who, when he leaves the room to look for her glasses, leans over and says, "And what do you think you're going to do while he's barking around?"

"No good deed goes unpunished," he moans in the car when I tell him what she said.

I'm furiously happy, for my tumor markers are rising and it's a race to squeeze every last joy out of life. Defiance is no longer the goad. Happiness is my protection, my talisman. I nestle in it. If I'm happy, I can't die. I can't be this sick—I'm too alive. Alive, and scrambled as they come. "Broaching middle age," I write after one weekend away, "I find myself attacked by the vulnerabilities of old age (only a few years left—how do you conduct a life?) and negotiating the teenage concerns of new sobriety, after years of hard drinking (what do you say to a stranger at a party, if you're not lit?). Confounding things more, I'm falling deeply in love. I'm coming alive, and I'm dying, and if that's not an unsettling state, I don't know what is." My emotional age is gerrymandered—I am twenty, I am fifty, I am thirty-seven, I am surely the same as seventy. Staring down into my own black hole, I am every age, and because of that, I worry I'll never fit easily with anyone.

"I'm so goddamn grateful to be alive and facing my thirty-eighth birthday," I write in the stillness, just before everything blows up. "I'm probably the only woman in the United States eager to reach forty. If I can just have ten more years—a decade's a lot, in the last one I loved, married, helped raise two kids, loved again, held interesting jobs, traveled all over, learned to be alone, learned I shouldn't be so alone, became more human, it was largely great—I can resign myself to an early death. Early? I'll be nearly fifty, that's not so tragically young."

I ride the streak till it starts to break, in (one for the remedial waking dreamer) Atlantic City. My magazine has sent me to cover Miss America. Even on the car ride down, the streak is giving out. The bolt now demands I keep myself straight as a splint, but there's two of us in the cramped backseat, no room. I bend, through absolute will, in perspiration, in agony. The bolt exacts punishment. I'm aching, drained, through the whole lousy weekend, in which the photographer is a jerk ("I cannot even bring myself to walk on that carpet," she announces at the hotel, and we all have to lug suitcases back onto the boardwalk and look for a place she can approve), the Misses, smiling rabidly, give useless, robotic answers in interviews, I get lost in the projects on the way to the restaurant, and Ben is testy on the phone. I've played my hand, it's pretty clear by Sunday noon, when we pull away from the Taj Majal.

The danger draws closer, its shadow jutting forward and almost, barely now, sweeping mine. Hurrying to elude its shadow, I fail to see I'm sprinting into the shade. But when Ben breaks up with me the Tuesday I get back, I couldn't be more in the dark.

On the morning when we get in the fight, I'm too jazzed with worry about the newest round of tumor markers—results in today, F's secretary predicts—to notice I'm pushing my luck over Saturday-night plans. Ben can't say if he can get together. He has to see how the writing goes, he says on the phone, voice taut but rising. That's one wait too many for me; I want to know now, and that's it. He's screaming—*he's not some yuppie lawyer who keeps regular hours; his commitment is to his work, he can't have a girlfriend*—I'm screaming right back, and then it's over. He's out.

He's not going anywhere, my friends advise when I tell them what happened. Secretly we all welcome the switch in problem. After nine intense months of end-game cancer, it's a relief to have something ordinary to analyze, like a boyfriend who's freaking out.

He'll be back, they say when I play them his follow-up breakup message on my answering machine.

Just blowing smoke, they say when I get the letter he's Fed-Exed, overnight service, from a hotel in L.A. "You'll always be on my mind," it grandly concludes. "I'll always be filled with love and admiration for you. I want you to know that I wish you well, and that you can always call on me in an emergency."

"But he dumped me during an emergency," I point out, and my friends answer, Well, you know, he's panicking. Don't worry. It's not over. I'm not worried, not a lot, because a while ago, I figured out a truth the advice books were clueless on—those fear-of-commitment guys, they never go away.

When the tumor markers come in, my friends hem or remain silent.

462.

Ben and I talk. We argue. I leave my machine on, break down, call him, learn he's screening, too. One night he shows up unexpectedly and rings the bell downstairs. "I can't," I tell the intercom and, returning to the couch, pick up my book. The words are blurry. I don't care. I make myself read every one.

In my apartment, four nights running, Otis Redding on a street-mix tape sings "Pain in My Heart." *I want you, girl, to come back, come back, come back*, he makes his voice stagger, in a pleasing cry of desperation. On other songs, there's evidence that Otis has been as poorly behaved as Ben, and regard—the man is, by his own account, broken, begging, down on his knees. *Pain in My Butt*, I sing along, laughing gleefully. But by the Sam Cooke portion, I'm more subdued. *That's it. I quit*, Sam Cooke crows. Two horns honk emphatically. *I'm moving on*, Sam Cooke declares. He sounds pretty sure.

On a crowded bus uptown, I find myself packed in next to Nancy, the ill-tempered one from the support group. How is everyone? I ask, warming with nostalgia, even though it's only been three months since I dropped out. I'd stopped attending after deciding life was too good and too short to consign one seventh of my evenings to cancer. Between the support group and the shrink, the social worker and the nutritionist, the illness was becoming a calling, and what was the point of working so hard to live if I wasn't going to have a life? I canceled the support group and the shrink.

Doris isn't doing well, Nancy tells me above the rush-hour squall. That is not a surprise. Hunched down against the ache in her liver, always in the same chair, Doris kept silent except to express regret for the many bad turns her life had taken. And neither, Nancy says, is Jane. *Jane?* I say—but Jane was hardly sick; she only had it in one lymph gland. Not anymore, Nancy says. Jane's cancer exploded and now it's everywhere: spine, lungs, even behind her eyes. They'd just switched her to Meges, too. Oh God, I say, swallowing against the hard metallic taste that's come into my mouth. And how are you? we ask each other nervously.

All right, we both shrug. Hanging in. But when Nancy pulls for her stop and begins moving toward the door, I notice a sideways dip in her walk. Looking down, I see she's leaning on a cane.

You're too suggestible, I admonish myself when, soon after, I acquire the dip. Come right over, F says, but X rays show nothing. Go home and we'll watch it, he says. He'll schedule an MRI to see what that reveals, but for now we'll have to go with what the X rays say: nothing.

The next morning, when it hurts too much to walk, fear squelches pride and I put in a call to Ben. He's there in no time, and for the next couple of days, he all but moves in—lies next to me on the bed, orders up food, makes me laugh with snarky comments about cheesy cable shows. When I touch him, though, he turns me down, and when he, in turn, reaches out to me, I refuse, in retaliation. I don't mind the limp or the stalemate so long as he's there, but when he leaves, despondence rams me. Nothing feels real anymore. My life is defined by what I can't have. I want everything to be okay and it won't be, not ever again. I want Ben. I want forgiveness, even if Claire's right and the illness isn't punishment, but life at its hardest. I want God to remove this. Cancer is blasphemy. Cancer is a pig, it's a greedy pig.

In this irreal state, it doesn't seem odd when the problem resolves on its own and I go from paralysis to the StairMaster again in under a week. In this irreal state, it seems normal when Ben does an about-face and asks my machine if I'll go to Europe with him. In this irreal state, it's not remarkable when F calls with the MRI results and says they've found a large tumor at the base of my spine, but not to worry—it's been there all along.

"There's nothing new here. This isn't progression," he says. "The lab just missed it before, for some reason. But the thing is, it's really very big. I mean, *big*. I'm amazed you're not in more pain."

"I am in more pain," I say.

"No, I mean, like, a *lot* of pain," he says.

"No, I mean, like, a *lot* of pain, too," I say, but pain doesn't signal action. Progression does. Until a new lesion appears on a scan, we're going to stay this course.

In Europe I had the illusion I'd outwitted the danger. I'd paid my money, made my escape, and if I guarded my body carefully—no sudden or broad moves—it could seem like I'd given the thing the slip. The trip was so good that, looking back, I think, for a time, I did.

On the lam, with Ben, I was ebullient. So was he. When he wasn't interviewing sources for his book, we did what we wanted. In London we called down for braised oxtail and ate room-service dinner in bed. We made a pilgrimage to Dickens's house and had high tea at a swank hotel where, we learned, a disgraced American pop singer was newly checked in. The man had recently been charged with perversity by a young boy who claimed intimate knowledge of certain identifying marks. "Think he gets the spotted dick for dessert?" Ben sniggered, and for the rest of the trip, the Brit-pudding joke could not fail to make us snort.

In Paris the manager of the Crazy Horse Saloon chased us, yelling, down the street after we tried to sneak a side-door peek at the bare-breasted dancers. In Vienna we were awestruck at the opera, moved by the arias in *Carmen* and the sophisticated dazzle of the crowd. Even in New York, at Lincoln Center, I'd never seen Japanese women in kimonos, or men quite so handsome in black tie.

It was only back in England, on a train up to Oxford, that the danger finally caught my scent. Without warning, an electric buzz tore down my leg, burning me so I wanted to scream. Instead, I turned white and for the rest of the trip trembled whenever a slight hum made me fear the current would zap me again.

Recrossing the Atlantic, two of us were in the seats, but there were three of us on the plane.

My first day back in the office, the managing editor was on a tear. I'd forgotten to assign a writer to a profile of an actress and the piece was scheduled to run. There wasn't time to get someone on the case. "You will have to write it yourself," she said, raising an eyebrow when I protested, "I can't. I'm way too jet-lagged." Not professional. The exhaustion I felt was terrifying—profound and conquering, unholy, nothing to do with time zones—but I couldn't tell her that. I had no acceptable excuse. Returning to my desk, I made arrangements to meet the actress at her apartment.

I took a car up and grunted out questions, came back down and typed up her answers, and all the while, inside and out, I was going gray. "I can't bend enough to get tights on anymore," I said in a scared, whispered call to F. "It hurts my hip to sit on the toilet. I have to lift myself up on my palms." But I just had an MRI that showed nothing, he said. He wouldn't worry. I'd had other episodes of impaired mobility, and they had corrected themselves.

For the first time, he didn't order a test.

The night everything went black, I was two paragraphs off from the end of the profile. I'd have finished the piece before leaving the office if I'd pushed, but I couldn't. The magazine's Christmas party was that evening. Attendance was required. At the antiquarian bookstore, I stood by the food table, too tired to seek out conversation or anyone I knew. After twenty minutes, I edged back through the crowd, found the coat check, fought the crush ascending the stairs, hailed a cab.

At home, in my living room, I accidentally dropped a piece of mail. The paper falling to the floor was like a prearranged signal. After months of straining against its leash, the fury of pain broke free and ripped into me as I bent down, slashing through my back, tearing into flesh, pressing without mercy onto bone. I bit back a cry. I grimaced. I struggled to make myself stand, and felt—heard—something rip in my back. Stunned, I sank to my knees, into the waiting shadow.

What happened next is still fairly unspeakable for me. It would take four more shrinks to recover the memories, and one would have to be a detonation specialist in order to blast through the morphine slag that's hardened over them all, and anyway, I'm not much interested. The following is the most I intend to remember. I have no desire to know more.

In what would be the last time I stood for two months, I forced myself to get up off the floor. The shadow was trying to suck me into darkness, but I willed myself not to faint. The floor was the only thing steady in the apartment. The bed, a long way off, was swaying out of vision, but I kept it in view, made it there, and on the way, even grabbed the headset of the cordless phone. A glimmer-thought had told me I would need it.

On the bed, a burning pain embraced me, seared me, like a girdle on fire. I could not move. I didn't test it, but I knew I couldn't walk. At three A.M., when I had to go to the bathroom, I found a glass and peed into that. At dawn, when I hadn't improved, I phoned F, who called for an ambulance. I shouted, cried, when the men shifted me onto the stretcher. They were breaking me! They couldn't! They had to, they did.

For the three weeks while they scanned and siphoned me in the New York hospital, I was drowning in pain. A cough was too much vibration. In bed I lined my body with pillows to keep myself still so I couldn't turn over in sleep. The cancer had devoured two vertebrae. A third collapsed when an orderly bringing me back from a scan fumbled and dropped me onto the mattress. Pain slammed me so hard then, I tried to scream but my mouth could only stretch wide, into an O. Pain had ripped out my voice.

In a morphine delirium, I sang the river, but the drug had the ability to bend its course. I was not moving anywhere. I was suspended. So was time. When the editor came to my room on Christmas Eve, carrying gifts, a couple for me, several to take home and wrap for her husband, I was surprised to learn it was no longer mid-December. Two weeks had passed. The editor told me that everyone on staff had heard, they were rooting for me. She invited me to spend Christmas with her, at her home. I was pleased to be asked, even if I wasn't going anywhere.

I wasn't going anywhere because I was in a dream. People could enter it when they wanted to, walk into it from their lives, but I had to stay there to spin it or we were all going to disappear. The editor darted in and out. So did Judy and Diego, Claire and Nicole, Anna, Michelle, my father, brother, everyone. My mother was there, on the telephone. You know the tremor you saw in my hand in Mexico, she said. Well, they found out what it was: Parkinson's. Ahhhhhh, I said, wanting to comfort her, but I was so busy keeping us all going. I had to imagine new things, or the edges of the world would curl.

Ben helped in the creation. Piling the bed with his favorite books, he read me into other visions. Once, floating down a side path, I returned to see him pacing my bedside, hunched over. He was Richard III. The day after Christmas, on New Year's Eve, he came by with party hats and poppers. At midnight he slid in beside me. After a while he covered my mouth so I wouldn't cry out, in pleasure. The old lady in the next bed was muttering and snoring, weaving her own dream.

The pain got worse. They kept bumping up the morphine, till one afternoon I nodded down, drooling onto my chest. Overdose. They cut back. The pain got worse. I was too ill to be moved, ever, from the bed. The nurses changed the sheets around me.

The pain got worse. The day after New Year's Eve, F came to tell me what they'd figured out: This was an emergency. I needed to begin the transplant right away. But the New York hospital didn't do transplants. Duke University, in Durham, North Carolina, did. The day after, men in jumpsuits came to my room and carefully slid me onto a stretcher. "Tell that driver to avoid the potholes," Ben shouted in the ambulance, on the way to the private plane.

"Hang on, Robobabe," he said once we were airborne, reaching down to smooth my hair. "Hang on."

At Duke they settled me into a bed in my own room, then instantly came with a wheelchair and tried to make me get out. "Honey, we have to scan you," the nurse said. But by now I couldn't sit up if I wanted. The tumors had frozen me into a fetal position. When the orderlies transferred me to the stretcher by lifting me up on the sheet, I cried and cursed them.

"You're days away from becoming a paraplegic," the doctors hurried in to say after they'd seen the scans. "The tumors are severing your spinal chord." It made no sense to start the transplant, they'd decided, if I was going to end up in a wheelchair. We needed to begin radiation immediately to shrink the tumors—tomorrow, if possible.

The pain got worse. Breath by itself could make it ripple and pulse. The tumors had broken through bone and into the spinal canal. My bones were cracking from within. That first night I begged: *Please, it has to stop, please help me, please, I need help.* The room was crinkly with morphine projections, but the pain cut through them. The morphine had put me in an Erskine Caldwell novel—we were all living out the desolation of Tobacco Road and my roommate from New York had come with us, the nurses had to flatten themselves to get around her, that old lady was crowding the room. The morphine had been able to tamper with the light, turn it eerie, but it couldn't touch the pain. It could no longer do the job. At three A.M. Ben screamed for a doctor. "You have to do something," he shouted. "She is in *world-class* pain." The night doctor prescribed Valium. I tried to warn him that

Valium would make me go out of my mind, but he couldn't understand me and it didn't matter. I was pretty far gone as it was.

"Congratulations!" I applauded the embarrassed-looking orderly who was wheeling me down to radiation. "Congratulations! I heard you got the part." People in the elevator looked at him, at me. They had not expected to encounter legendary style diva Diana Vreeland on their way to visit a relative. "I was delighted to hear," I said in my imperial Valium voice. "I have always believed that talent like yours *should* be rewarded."

"You have to lie flat," the radiation technologist pled, but I was hardwired into a curl. It was torture to unbend. The first three times on the table, I cried and trembled when they made me straighten out onto my back. On the fourth day, when I could unroll my body easily, I wept, with relief. The radiation was working.

The pain got better. Ben left, Judy appeared. She'd taken a week off from work to fly down and sleep by my bed, in a chair. One night we ordered up pizza and a VCR. "Your selections are *The Bodyguard* or *How to Clean Your Catheter*," she said. "Which one do you want?"

We went with Whitney Houston, but I could have used the cleaning film. Sometime in the small of the dream night, they'd snuck me out of the room and installed another port in my chest.

My aunt from Leesburg took Judy's place in the chair. We listened to classical music tapes, then my sister was there. She and Phil were now living in North Carolina. The first time, she brought their son, who was three. He held out a cookie. "He thinks it will make you better," she said. When the catheter got infected and my fever spiked 102, she held a blow-dryer to me, set on cool.

A physical therapist came to teach me how to walk. "Way to go," my main nurse, Henry, cheered when she saw me teetering in the hall. Henry was from Kentucky. "You know how I know that attitude plays a big part in whether you get better?" she'd muse, checking the Vancomycin drip. "Back in Kentucky, I was working on the mental ward when one of the schizophrenics got lung cancer. That state's so poor, they'd only pay to treat one—schizophrenia or cancer—not both. We didn't have a choice. It had to be his mind. The guy was a three-pack-a-day smoker, so we all ganged up on him, explained he had cancer, told him he had to quit, but he was too schizophrenic to get it. He kept on smoking, and they never treated him. Ten years later, he's still alive. I think he's alive because he's just too out of it to understand he's supposed to die."

Radiation ended. The transplant didn't begin. "We're going to have to wait, because of the infection you had," the head doctor said. "You might as well go home and try this new hormone, see how you do." He wrote me out a prescription for a drug called Cytadren.

Nurse Henry helped me pack my stuff. My parents had driven down. I needed a walker to get to the car, but I had no trouble folding myself in. I could bend, twist, do anything I wanted, because toward the dawn of the long morphine night, the pain, thank God, had disappeared.

At my parents' I saw that Parkinson's had changed my mother's gait. When she walked across a room, she slid her feet, as if she were polishing the floor with cloth shoes.

My mother shuffled. I got by on a cane. At lunch my father would take us to a strip-mall Chinese restaurant and, after parking the car, go in by himself. He had learned the hard way not to try and help us navigate the distance.

"Stuart, I can do it," my mother would say sharply, spurning his offer of an arm.

"Dad, I am just fine," I'd sigh.

Soon my father made sure to stride briskly toward the restaurant, never looking back. *Of course*, his march said, *I just assume you're right behind me.* Then he'd watch from a window as we tottered toward the door, making little eeping sounds on the ice.

The first month back in New York, I stayed inside. You would not believe this blizzard, my friends had all said on the phone my last week in the hospital. You should see the city! We are snowed under! My friends had not been exaggerating. In New York the sidewalks were thin slushy lines cutting through huge white canyons. On my street, snow was banked higher than a man's head. Even people without canes had trouble getting around.

New York looked different, and in the precise light of February, so did my apartment—smaller, the way your elementary-school room would if you had reason to go back. My body, too, was not the same. Things had happened to it in the night. Some were easy to detect. All I had to do was stand on the scale to see I'd lost fifteen pounds. Others required attention and wits.

Though I'd grown thin, my waist had widened dramatically, three inches bigger at least. I did not determine for days that this mystery was linked to another—the puzzle of why the kitchen pots, formerly hung within grabbing distance over the stove, were all out of reach—until passing the hallway mirror one morning, I stopped and did a double take. Didn't I used to be taller? I did, the measuring tape confirmed. After fifteen years of being five feet seven, I'd dropped to five-five, a result of the three collapsed vertebrae. The belly roll was a question of physics. Since matter can only be displaced, not erased, the loss in height had translated to a gain around my middle.

These night changes were proof: From irreal, it's a short leap to surreal. Body reshapes itself, as if you've just stepped out of a fun-house mirror—now, that is Dada-life. Friends who called were leading real lives, no prefixes. They couldn't understand. I thought about going back to the support group, but when I phoned Jean, I found out I couldn't. All but one of the women had died.

Once I knew where to look, the alterations in my body were obvious. The differences in my psyche were harder to measure. They could only reveal themselves over time, through reflection or inference. When I first went back to work, in March, I would have said I was exactly the same. Demonstrably better, in fact.

"One twenty!" F's secretary called to report the first week. A hundred twenty? One miracle appeared to have sparked another. As rapidly as they'd climbed, my tumor markers were plummeting.

"Ninety!" she phoned a month later. "Keep going. All you have to do is get to thirty."

"Sixty!" The drop continued another month, then stalled. Fifty-seven. Fifty-nine. When my assistant next buzzed to say, "F's office on the line," I wasn't even sure what it was about.

"You're normal!" the secretary exclaimed.

"What?" I asked, distracted by a deadline. I was normal?

"You are twenty-seven," she said. "You, my dear, are normal."

My mouth fell open. I didn't care if someone caught me crying at my desk. Let them ask. "Take a look!" I'd shout. "Can't you see? I'm freaking normal!"

A week later, as I was walking down the street, a sentence came into my head. Oh, I thought casually, almost distractedly. I'm going to live.

The internal changes started to become obvious. They surfaced in my relationship with Ben. We'd had a sweet romance, so long as I was docile. The whole time we'd been in love, the illness had kept me gentled, but I wasn't actively ill anymore.

In Europe Ben hadn't thought twice about telling me to change my clothes before we went out. "I think you should find something a little more attractive to wear," he'd suggested before a dinner with friends in Paris, and without hesitation, I did. Now, when he tried this, I thought he was out of line.

"I'm not saying those jeans make your ass look fat, but I think you should put something else on," he'd said when I returned from Duke. Me, I didn't. For one thing, the only public appearance we were planning to make was at a deli. For another, his butt was bigger than mine, so why didn't he go change his pants? I kept quiet on the second point, but I kept my jeans on. He sulked all night.

A friend pointed out that we were fighting all the time now. I probably didn't realize it, she said. Why didn't I keep a diary, she suggested. I'd see.

The diary confirmed her observation, but it couldn't tell me what to do. My instincts could have, but I ignored them until, eventually, fear overrode me. With each successive argument, I became more afraid that if I stayed, I was going to get sick again. It'd be years before a doctor would say to me, succinctly, "Your cancer has always been connected to loss," but I already grasped that and I sensed I was about to lose. Maybe it's better to cut your losses now, I thought, coming home from another rancorous night.

When things blew up again—on the street, so loud, we'd attracted rubberneckers—I took a breath and quietly said, "Maybe we should put some space between us."

"Fine," he growled. "Let's put ten years' space between us."

At the final moment, he managed to do what he'd said he'd wanted to the first night. He stopped time. I stared at him forever, and in that eternity, I considered what to do. I knew he didn't mean what he'd said. I knew I loved him as profoundly as I'd loved anyone, beyond cause or sense. But I also knew we couldn't be in love if I was dead, and no one had been able to convince me I hadn't gotten breakup cancer.

This was looking to be a protracted breakup. If I kept it short, I stood a chance.

"You're right," I answered. "Okay."

I almost said something else, but I stopped.

And turned.

And I walked away.

It was hard, but I called the river; its currents eddied into a pond. For the longest time, my life remained unruffled, despite daily sorrow over Ben. My tumor markers stayed down. Once more, I switched oncologists. "There's someone new here at Sloan Kettering I think you'd really like," Jean said. "She just came over from Italy."

It took a few visits before I realized Chiara Antonelli was the smartest woman I'd ever met. It took only one to know I did, indeed, really like her. "Say no more," she said when I told her that the reason I was leaving F was his insistence I wouldn't make ten more years. "He's a strict numbers guy," I said. "When I ask him about my chances, he just shakes his head. Just, No. I understand he doesn't want to give me false hope. But if he doesn't realize there are exceptions to the statistics, he either hasn't been practicing long enough or he's not that good."

"I know exactly the kind you mean," she said with a half grin. Small and fine-boned, with wide brown eyes, she looked both impish and elegant, despite a stained white doctor's smock. "Let me explain one thing. I don't just want to treat you for breast cancer. I'm looking to cure you of breast cancer."

She was aware, and so was I, that there was no such thing as a cure at my stage, not by official medical reckoning. The most doctors are allowed to say if Stage 4 cancer disappears is that the patient is N.E.D.: no evidence of disease. A cure implies forever, and with cancer that has spread, no doctor can promise that. She wasn't making any promises. She was alluding to the new treatments coming down the pike, giving a nod to hope. She was telling me, most important, that we were looking in the same direction.

Antonelli was idealistic, interesting—studying for her Ph.D. in philosophy on the side, she said—and she made me laugh. I couldn't sign up fast enough. But first she made me agree to one thing: "At the first sign of a change on your scans, you will have the bone marrow transplant."

For two years nothing changed on the scans. I began to believe nothing ever would. But, of course, one day everything did.

"You promised," Antonelli reminded me.

"But it's just a tiny spot," I wailed. "It might not even be progression. Come on! You even said it. It could be delayed healing showing up."

"We agreed," she said.

I refused. I couldn't. Things were too good. I turned on her, furious, but then behind me I heard it, the universal sound, made specific and exact. Antonelli spoke, sympathetic. "I know," she said. "It will be hard. I know." Reluctantly I joined her and the struggle was in the song. We sang the preparations, the chemo, and the injections. We sang through the spring and summer, into the fall, when I entered the hospital and the transplant began.

PART THREE

VARIATIONS ON MY ROOM IN THE BONE MARROW UNIT: IN THE ROOM OF COWS

Marc Chagall's peasant is milking a red jersey cow
incessantly, letting flow a river of cream across
a muddy floor. Here is a peaceable kingdom of cows,
Danish next to Holstein next to Swiss. The bulls have had
their testosterone lowered with medication and now lie meekly
with the skittish rest of the herd. They no longer bang
their steaming heads against the barn wall when I enter.
The hospital nurse in a cow uniform keeps trying
to tie us into blue gowns, taking advantage of our new
docility. This room is as large as a field but is still
a room. It opens with a double-hinged hospital door.
I sit in a corner, at a drugstore soda counter, having
a coffee milk shake. After blessing the cow and coffee bean,
I lace the shake with my latest prescription, a syrup
for mouth sores, a Christmas gift from my pharmacist.
A Holstein serves me, like Elsie in her apron, and a Longhorn
tries to pick me up, but he is easy to resist.
I prefer men, though I know there are other options.
Chagall says hello, but isn't interested in females without hair,
however jewel blue and red my scarf is. After my shake,
I sleep on clean heaped straw. A nurse hooks
me up to an IV of chocolate milk, vitamin fortified.
She gossips of great bulls she has known, steamy nights
of alfalfa and Merlot with a Beefmaster in Vegas;
and that recent ménage à trois with the Angus brothers
in a pole barn. I make up some travels to India, and a tryst
with a Brahman bull as she checks all my lines:
IV tubes flowing in, and Foley catheter running out.

—Julie Moulds

FIGHT

ON THE OCCASION OF MY FIRST HAIRCUT AFTER THE TRANS-plant, I threw a fit in the middle of Barneys' hair salon, stopped the cut in progress, and asked for the manager. I wanted to see him, I told the receptionist. Now.

"It was supposed to be a tiny, tiny trim. Not layers," I said. "I'd said, 'Hardly anything at all,' and now—look! look!—he cut it into a ball."

"Honestly, I think it's cute," the manager said gently. "But have a seat. Let me see what I can do." His manner soothed me, and by the time he'd finishing brushing off the last stray hairs, I'd calmed down enough to think maybe he'd been right. And that maybe it wasn't the cut that was off.

"I'm really sorry," I said. "I overreacted, I know, but I, um, I should say, I was on chemo all last year—I had, uh, a—"

"Oh, you should have told us," the manager said. "We would have understood."

They may have, but I didn't, not till the next day, when it dawned on me that I thought I'd personally grown that hair, every strand, through the force of sheer goddamn will. More than a trim, and the hairdresser was not only messing with my work, he was taking me back.

"I don't care. I kind of like having no hair. Maybe I'll just go around bald," I'd told the new cancer support group on my first visit, in early spring the year before. My week had been given over to advance work for chemo: one test, then another, then, sorry, one more. With each new test, there's a new doctor who reviews my chart. Age thirty-two: lump first detected. Thirty-three: lumpectomy, chemo, radiation. Thirty-seven: recurrence to the spine, paralysis, emergency airlift to Duke Medical Center, terror, radiation, relief.

Age thirty-nine. New area of calcification revealed on bone scan. Consensus reached that hormone therapy of two years be discontinued and preparations for a bone marrow transplant begun. Admission into transplant program not guaranteed, of course. Six to eight months of warm-up chemotherapy required first. If regression can be proven on a scan, patient may fork over a sum in the low six figures for four high-dose chemo bombs—to be brought to the point of death and back four times.

Transplant will be conducted on an outpatient basis, except for hospitalizations for high-dose infusions or infection. Patient planning to have live-in care, as well as to strut around town with her bad, bald head hanging out. Or so she pretends to her support group.

"Really? You like losing your hair?" they ask. "You like it when it's winter and your head gets cold? Or when your eyelashes fall out into your eyes? You like losing your hair all over? Oh, *interesting.*"

Nobody's really buying the cancer warrior act, not even when I announce that maybe I'll get a big tattoo on my head and go out like that. But after two years on hormones, ever aware they can only hold back metastatic disease for so long, I am bristling, ripped, aching to do battle. I want at it.

Ever since we decided, I've been fighting mad. I was fighting mad when a thick nurse can't find a vein and asks a series of pointless questions. ("Do you have lymphodema because of an operation?" No, I got it because I tore my lymph glands out with my teeth.) Fighting mad when I go to an uptown salon to see about a wig, and the stylist unfurls some socialite's hairpiece ("She's the most sophisticated woman in New York, and she's only going to use this for four nights!") and tells me I'll have to cough up $5,500, minimum, if I want similar coverage. "I don't know where they're getting their hair," he sniffs when I observe that other places are asking a grand.

Fighting mad when a writer, unhappy over news that her daughter is dyslexic, calls and says, "You'll understand this. If you're not perfect in this world, they think you're not worth considering."

"Every other conversation I have lately is prefaced by the words 'You'll understand this,'" I tell the group. "Especially if the subject's calamity. What, because I have cancer, I automatically understand all manner of suffering and injustice? If I hear one more person say, 'You're an inspiration,' I'm going to slap them silly."

If the bell doesn't go off soon, I will.

The fight is a ribbon of fire running through me. Burning to go, to bound into the ring, I've been forced to abandon the happiness program. The word *happiness* derives from the same root as *happen*. If you're happy, you let things happen, and I can't do that now—give myself over, see how it goes? That could be costly. If I'm lax, I won't be prepared. And I must be prepared at all times, because no one can say exactly when I'll have to be ready.

"You'll need four or five rounds of preconditioning chemo before we can decide. Maybe more," John Lambrakis, the head of the transplant program, said when we met. This variety of chemo, Taxol, was milder than the kind before, he said. I'd have hair loss and fatigue, yes. Bone pains, some days, and on those I'd take Dilaudid. But not the terrible nausea.

"How many more?" I asked.

"Tough to say. Could be seven. Or eight."

By the time the support group convenes again, I've had one.

"How'd it go?" chirps the group leader, the Reverend Jacqui, cocking her head and peering at me like a bird. A mail-order minister, Reverend Jacqui began running groups for rape victims and cancer patients after her acting career hit the skids. Her sharply cheerful demeanor doesn't disturb me so much, or even the part where she asks everyone to close her eyes and "Feel the yes! current." But after one of the women told me that Reverend Jacqui once made everyone lie on the floor and envision their own funerals, I've been uneasy.

"She actually had everyone imagine they were dead?" I said. "Isn't that the opposite of that approach where cancer patients imagine themselves getting better?" Isn't that, by the principles of imaging, like bumping people off? Reverend Jacqui, I'm concerned to note, takes a particular interest in our pain.

"Fine," I tell her now. "Chemo went okay. I even went hiking in the mountains two days after." Susan calls my bluff.

"Maybe that's what I did wrong," she cracks. "Maybe I should have gone mountain climbing."

"If I were having chemo again, I know it would be worse," Judith sighs. "Since cancer, my life is one cumulative loss. If I have to have a tooth out, I see it as a loss."

"I don't feel like it's cumulative loss," I say. "If anything, a lot of my life seems like cumulative gain."

"I would be very careful with a thought like that," Reverend Jacqui interrupts, displeased by the direction this talk is taking. "When I find myself thinking something like that, I ask myself what it's about. Usually there's another thought behind it." Her eyes are shiny. She wants the pain. What a vampire, I think.

Support groups proliferated in the nineties, after a study by a doctor named David Spiegel showed that women with advanced breast cancer who enrolled lived twice as long as those who didn't. But no one ever cites a follow-up study that found that groups that weren't run according to Spiegel's model had little effect on health. And poorly run ones, I'm beginning to suspect, will only make you *feel* like you're living longer. I like the women in this one—a couple of artists, a jazz guitarist who's off to tour Senegal, a shrink, another editor—but if I have to see much more of Reverend Jacqui, I can't vouch for her life span.

Over the next couple of weeks, I order in provisions, lay up supplies against the siege (but whether that means me against cancer or cancer against me, I'm not sure). I buy new shower liners, a pink plastic bucket, a lamp with a base like a tree. Coriander hand cream, two light-green hat boxes for scarves and caps, a rug for the living room, a side table for the sofa. I have a vague notion that, while I'm home, people will be dropping by for drinks and conversation. For those off-hours when I'm not entertaining, I stockpile books, many of them about the Middle Ages, when life was brutish and people had to know how to fight.

I bring in a rented StairMaster for the long summer ahead, for days when I don't feel like going to the gym. I cushion my place with new upholstery, get an air conditioner, make appointments—for tune-ups, for dental fillings, for a wig.

"I gotta be honest with you . . . I hate people on time. I'm only kidding you!" says Joe the wig man when I show up late. The son of an Italian barber, he runs a hair shop in the theater district. "You want to wear that," he says, pointing to a ferocious head-dress he's constructing for *Beauty and the Beast*, "I'll give it to you for free. I'm only kidding you!"

On the wall there's a framed poster with little oval portraits of all the presidents, leaving off at Nixon. Someone's drawn a rug on Franklin D. Roosevelt. Joe tries a long auburn wig on me for size. "Hey! You look good as a redhead." As he works, he reminisces about the time, twenty years ago, when the Italians were trying to pass off Russian hair as Italian. Soviet locks were embargoed back then. He didn't mind the scam. "Russian hair—there's nothing like it," he says. "When people are hungry, their hair grows better."

Joe matches samples to my head. He estimates the cost. ("We charge good-looking people more. I'm just kidding you!") About fifteen hundred dollars, he figures. I forget to ask him where my new hair's from.

Korea, guesses Giacomo, the stylist I take the wig to, but after one wearing, I beg to differ. No Korean woman I've ever seen has hair this insane. There's a little secret no one lets new cancer patients in on, and that's that they'll be expected to master someone else's hair problems instantly, even though it probably took them twenty-five years to get a fix on their own. After one walk in the rain, I decide that whoever's hair this was had had it all cut off rather than deal with its demonic-possession problems, including frizzies so determined, they border on the psychotic. I buy a curling iron and a stand and gamely have a go at it, but mostly, I decide, I'll wear the Black Muslim cap with synthetic bangs Giacomo tosses in for free.

Around this time, I vow again not to be like one of those cancer patients who worries about her hair and weight—i.e., all the ones who aren't dead. And I fail, repeatedly. "I know this is a stupid question, but did you, uh, lose weight?" I inquire of former transplant patients in the kind of tone that's generally used to ask, "So where do people get drugs around here?" "I wondered that myself," they usually answer. "Like, ten pounds."

My resolve is perversely helped by one of the doctors I see for a checkup. "What is that?" the gynecologist asks. She gestures toward my rounded stomach, visible where the robe's fallen open. "It wasn't there last time."

"That," I say, "is fat," explaining about the side effects of the hormone therapy and the crash of the three vertebrae.

"It may be hormones, and it may be you need a little extra going into this, but I also think that's from your diet," she says. "When this is over, you may want to start watching calories."

"I already do!" I protest. "I work out five times a week, forty-five minutes on the StairMaster."

"But do you do stomach exercises? They'll help your muscle tone," she says.

I stare at her like she's just reached over and conked me on the head. I'm facing a procedure that kills 10 percent of the people who undergo it, because I have a condition that leaves 80 percent dead in five years, and she's suggesting I work on my abs. Yeah, right, let me whip out my to-do list here. *Buy organic carrots, take shoes to be reheeled, have bone marrow transplant, do crunches.* Check. Where do women get these crazy ideas about having to be perfect in every way? Now we know: during Pap smears. The exam hurts. "Lack of estrogen," she says when I yelp. From the hormone treatment. "And you haven't been having sex. If you don't use it, you lose it. You'll need a lot of lubricant when you do." Oh, wait, let me put that down, too: *Buy KY, extra large; get boyfriend; fuck him.*

At the front desk, I decline when the receptionist wants to schedule a six-month appointment. Silently thanking this doctor for the sudden clarity, I walk out of her office for good.

When, ten days after the first treatment, the hair starts to go, it's brutal. I'd figured it would be easier the second time around. It isn't. Hair loss is one of the hardest aspects of chemotherapy, most patients agree, and that's because everything else reprises a familiar, if unpleasant, experience. We've all had sore throats; we've all been tired; we've all thrown up before. But in the natural universe, hair generally doesn't fall out with a sudden, horrifying thud of force. Chemo's hailstorm of hair appears to signal the body that it's in grave danger; the body, in turn, panics right down to its DNA and provokes a kind of flight-or-fight response in the psyche. The patient, who a week earlier was probably keeping herself relatively well wrapped, looks in the mirror at the scraggly remaining patches and thinks, Oh. My. God. I am seriously ill.

My God, you know, I really *might* die.

At least that's what I'm thinking on a Sunday in March as I stare at myself, now tonsured—bald on top but fringed, like a monk. What I say out loud is "Fucking butt cancer. You're not even breast cancer. You're butt cancer. A pain in the ass."

But there's no one there to shoot me a glance, to roll her eyes. And I can't, because I'm starting to cry.

Jungle animals prowl my dreams. At night, in my sleep, the illness takes the guise of a cat. Usually it's a lion, sometimes a cougar. Once, it isn't a cat at all, but a snake that stalks me, an anaconda—loosely, an anagram for cancer. "Cat" is a variant of "kat," the first three letters of my name. The wild cats represent the illness, which is a wild part of me.

Walking down a road in a game preserve, I see people racing toward me. "Mountain lion!" they shout. "Run!" Sprinting, I turn off onto a path that veers to the right. I know it will lead to safety.

When the danger is too savage or close, I become an observer, not even in the dream. *A girl stands alone on an African veldt. Suddenly a lion springs out at her from the bush. A rifle cracks and the cat falls dead. The girl is saved. But soon another lion, older and weaker, ambles into the clearing. The girl turns and laughs it to death.*

The two lions are the two episodes. The rifle shot is chemotherapy. The feeble state of the second animal, the recurrence, is a vote of confidence from my subconscious. The laughter is a reference to a book I've just read, Norman Cousins's classic *Anatomy of an Illness*, published in 1979. In it Cousins detailed the role laughter played in his prolonged recovery from a serious degenerative condition called ankylosing spondylitis. "I had a fast-growing conviction that a hospital was no place for a person who is seriously ill," Cousins wrote. With his doctor's blessing, he checked himself out and into a hotel, where he watched hours of *Candid Camera* and Marx Brothers films. After finishing the book, I've gone out and purchased some humor anthologies, placed them on top of the medieval series.

One thing about the dreams is consistent. Without fail, they tell me that this round, I'll be okay.

Lambrakis and Antonelli send me for a relay of procedures and tests. I go into the hospital for day surgery, come out with a familiar bump under my chest. A neat row of stitches runs across catheter number three. With its multiple lines of scars, my chest is beginning to resemble a boardgame.

Medical assistants call, schedule other appointments, various exams of my heart and lungs, several biopsies of my bones and bone marrow. The exams are to determine if I'm up to a transplant. The bone biopsy is to prove I have cancer.

"I think we may have established that already," I tell Antonelli. My cancer file weighs ten pounds.

Right, she says, but they need documentation. For the protocol. Seems once or twice, bone marrow transplants have been performed on people who, it turned out, didn't actually have cancer. Oops. Now, though the odds of this happening are slim, all transplant applicants have to submit fresh proof of cancer; i.e., a biopsy or two. At the suggestion of in-house counsel, I assume.

Maybe transplants don't have better track records, I speculate, because three quarters of the patients die from the stress of trying to get one. And I've been lucky; I haven't had to battle an insurance company that's denying payment on the grounds that the procedure is experimental.

The bone extraction sounds bad. The bone marrow aspiration is, I know for sure. My memory of the one I had at Duke is hazy. But F's description of the procedure isn't. "Basically, we break your hip in two places and go in with a needle," he'd said.

I stall. Antonelli lets me slide for a while, ambushes me by phone one morning. "Lambrakis and I were just talking," she says, adopting a casual tone that would not trick a three-year-old. "And we thought, Hey!, why don't you just come in today, get that bone marrow biopsy over with?"

Nooooo, I reply. I'm pretty busy.

"Come on," she says. "I'll do it myself. I've been told I'm pretty good."

I can't, I say. I've left those sedatives she prescribed for a past MRI at home; I'd probably need them. I've forgotten who I'm talking to. She can rustle up a few more for me, no problem, by two, which is when she'll expect to see me.

At the Breast Center, at two, at the blond-wood circle of a desk, the receptionist hands me an envelope with some tablets inside. I take them, find a chair, start each time a name is called. It's always two in, nurse and patient, one out, by herself. One woman emerges belching loudly—disgusting, except, *Oh God,* she's not, I am for casting her a look, because, *Jesus, she's talking through her throat.* At the desk, a Russian woman asks for a translator. She stumbles over words, but not because of her accent. She's missing part of her tongue. Volunteers in maroon coats circle with trays of pretzels and vanilla wafers, some too insistently helpful, all cancer patients themselves. A middle-aged couple settle down beside me. He pulls a sandwich from his briefcase. It's three o'clock.

Ten minutes after I'm called into the examining room, Antonelli arrives. Her appearance relaxes me. In an eggshell-blue cashmere sweater and plaid slacks beneath white lab coat, she doesn't look like she wants to break anyone's bones. She looks like she just wants me to get up on the table, facedown. I can do that. The sedative's gone to my head. Hey, great sweater! Hey, how is she? And, man, how are those philosophy studies? That's really something she's doing there, going for a Ph.D. at night. Wow. I'm as convivial as they come, till she swabs my hip and I tense. The lidocaine's cold. I was wrong. I can't do this. "Right now I'm studying contemporary moral philosophy," she says, injecting the local. "One of its more fascinating themes is the role of luck in morality," she expounds, drilling down through bone. "Consider the drunk driver," she says above the lambent pain. "Is he less responsible if he hits someone on a street but, luckily, that person survives?" The pressure in my hip intensifies, and I moan. "I guess she doesn't want to hear any more about contemporary moral philosophy," she says to her assistant. The pressure ebbs; my hopes rise. It's over? No, it's the finale; a severe suctioning pain. "Shit," I cry. "Finished!" she shouts exultantly. Her assistant rubs my arm. "Finished!" she repeats, and thank goodness, it is.

As far as biopsies go, bone marrow is a romp compared to bone, which takes place a week later. For two hours, groggy but too awake, I whimper while the doctor extracts bone chips from my lower vertebra, except when he hits a nerve ending, and I scream.

The reports come back Agoddamnplus. Unfreakingbelievable. "The bone biopsy was negative," Antonelli says. "They couldn't find cancer. I think lots of places on the scan we thought were cancer aren't. They're scars from the old disease. Both your bone marrow biopsy and bone biopsy were negative. I'm very pleased." Me, I'm a little too psychically scarred from years of cancer roto-rooting to allow myself to get too happy just yet. The oncological good news always has a punch line.

Within minutes, it's delivered. Plans for the transplant aren't being scrapped, despite the encouraging results. Some malignant cells are still skulking around, Antonelli suspects. She wants to be cautious, proceed as planned. Fine with me, I tell her. Bomb the shadows. I'm happy to blast any weak cancer balls that are left.

"Good," she says. "But, I'm so sorry, you'll have to have one more bone biopsy. We still need the proof."

When I tell them the news about the negative returns, friends scream, "All right!"

"Keep doing exactly what you've been doing," they applaud.

I want to, but I've been investigating so many alternative treatments on the side, I'm not sure what, exactly, that would be. Perhaps it's the nutritionist's regimen of supplements, almost eighty tablets a day: vitamins A, D, E, and C; shark's cartilage; cat's claw pills; CoQ 10, powdered garlic, ginger, bromelaine, argenine; spirulina, glutamine, pycnogenol, melatonin, astragalus, echinacea, and selenium.

"Selenium?" the Chinese M.D. says when I hand him my list. "Don't take selenium. It causes breast cancer." He hands me back four Baggies full of dried leaves and knobby buds that brew up into a bitter tea. Maybe the Chinese herbs set me right.

Or maybe it was the prayers of Brother Henry, in Chicago. "Write to him," a friend said. "A friend of my mother's did. The woman had tumors in her liver. They'd given her no hope. But she got in touch with this guy and, I swear, her cancer totally disappeared." Or maybe those of the Sisters of Holy Name, in St. Louis, to whom I'd also written, having heard they ran a mean prayer list.

Or the purple drops sold by a mysterious cowboy in Casper, Wyoming. Someone knew someone whose father had taken them and had been snatched back from the abyss. Five hundred and eighty bucks for three jars, enough for the nightly foot soak that streaks my bathtub violet and turns my toes black.

Or the imaging tape that suggests telling the cancer, "Thank you for allowing me to learn the lessons I need to learn, but you can go now. You're not needed anymore." Good manners—all right. It appeals to the WASP in me. Or the chi gong healing exercise classes I've been taking down in Chinatown. Or the ankh that an astrologer I'd once edited mailed me from Egypt. "It's been dipped in the Nile," the attached note said. "Very powerful medicine."

Or the exercise, or the enforced-happiness good-attitude approach, or the periodic flirtations with an organic, vegetarian diet.

Or, could be, it was all the doing of Avi Scheinberg, spiritual healer from Israel. When he's in town, he operates out of an apartment in one of those flash-and-glass, hastily constructed buildings from the late eighties. In the waiting room, one wall is hung with paintings in the Time-Life Mystic Places genre—crudely rendered eyes superimposed on trees, that kind of thing, clearly Avi's work. The eyes appear to be gazing across the room at what looks like a Chinese restaurant wall of fame: lots of generic actor headshots, presumably satisfied customers. The only face I recognize is Arlo Guthrie's.

Avi's a popular guy. On this visit, three other clients are ahead of me. All look resigned to not going anywhere soon. The wait gives me time to page through a photo album pasted with testimonial letters. There's one from Vanna White, a vague thanks-for-everything note. I wonder about what her ailment was, carpal tunnel syndrome from letter turning?

I was skeptical and amused my last visit to Avi's, a year ago, when the herbalist insisted I go. This time I'm skeptical and a little repulsed, both with him and myself. But I'm back because the transplant is looming, and I'm starting to become really afraid, and right after the last time, my tumor markers fell to normal. Okay, I'd just been put on the new hormone, Cytadren, but what if? Just what if? What if a grifter like Avi is onto something, despite himself? I try to pretend that I'm here on a lark. What am I out, two hundred dollars and a bit of dignity? What does it matter? But it does. I'm ashamed of myself for behaving like a desperate cancer patient, an easy target for any charlatan who hangs out an eye-tree painting.

When the assistant finally brings me into the converted bedroom, Avi shows me where to hang my jacket. He covers the examining table with paper, invites me to lie down. Just like last time, he passes his hands over me and a ticklish current runs across my body. The hairs on my arm rise. "Feels like ants, right?" he says. Just last time, I twist my head to check his hands. They're empty. I'm sure this is a trick, but I can't figure it. The only clue is an occasional rustling of the paper near my head, as if Avi is reaching under the covering for something.

Fifteen minutes later, the ants trail off. Avi busies himself at his desk while I put my jacket back on. He holds his hand out, toward a chair. I take a seat. He says something in a thick accent that I can't quite catch, something like "Your body was angry for energy."

"*Angry?*" I say.

"No. *Hungry.* Your body was *hungry* for energy. Now I see that your aura has turned from white to blue."

"Is that good?"

"Yes," he says dismissively, apparently tired of truth seekers with all their questioning of the obvious.

He opens the file he's kept on me, asks about recent developments.

"If you got better after last time," he says, "why did you stop?"

Because you told me you learned how to do this when you were captured by UFOs, I consider saying, but don't. What if? Not what if he's onto something, but what if I get desperate again, so desperate I decide to come back?

Or, as it turns out, it was none of the above. "They found some malignant cells," Antonelli says two weeks later, after my second bone biopsy.

My smile drops. My shoulders, too. What a moron, what an impossibly stupid idiot, getting puffed up and convincing myself I was cured like that. Because as soon as she says this, I realize I had.

"No, it's good," she rushes to reassure me, seeing the look on my face.

I exhale hard through my nose. I don't answer.

"But now you have a better chance of getting accepted into the transplant," she says. "No, really, it's good."

The good times are coming.

Good and ready.

Good enough.

Good is the last thing I'd call it.

PUP

ALL GOOD NEWS IS RELATIVE, I DECIDE. MY FIRST LOVE ever calls me up. That's good. He's getting engaged. That's relative. Good for her, I guess. Probably for him, too, although he doesn't sound too certain.

When we broke up, when I was nineteen, on a study-abroad program in France, it was messy and I was naive. "I swear on my father's grave I'm not cheating on you," he'd said when we were lying together in his room and a beautiful French girl came knocking at the door. But he swore, I told my friends, when they became an item. *"Quel salaud,"* I learned to curse.

I've gotten together with him one night since, last fall, after he found my name in the alumnae bulletin. Over dinner I was spellbound again. His cheekbones were still beautifully curved. His voice was still slow and sleepy, but his mind darted and gleamed. I was a guppy again in tropical waters. We discussed literature and biology. He'd been reading a book about the brain. I had good taste at nineteen, I thought, surprised.

"My girlfriend is pretty and smart, but we don't talk like this," he'd said on the street, after the waiters had to blink the lights three times to get us to leave. I was giddy when I went upstairs. I was sure he'd call the next day. *He will: He talks better with me.* He didn't. He returned to California. I hadn't heard from him since, till now.

"Really?" I say on the phone, swallowed up for a moment in the flood of waters. He could have come back, I thought he might, return and allow me to start over where I first went wrong. Fly black and pluck me out of this grimness.

"Once I realized I equated marriage with death, it was easier. I'm taking baby steps," he says, and the fantasy I've simmered for a year goes flat. I don't want somebody who uses tinny pop-psych phrases like "baby steps" rescuing me.

"If we're only engaged a year and I can't go through with it, at least I will have made her happy for that year," he says, not sounding like a man convinced. He's considering taking baby steps away, at the last minute. I wonder when she'll figure it out: All good news is relative.

Superstition allows me to move. Two mornings running, "I Will Survive" is playing on the radio when I wake. An omen, I let myself think. Earlier in the spring, when signs appeared everywhere and even a bad horoscope could sink me for the day, I began to choose my portents carefully. A song could be prophetic. The news of the death of two bone marrow transplant patients at a cancer center out west couldn't be, too strong. In June all the papers had carried the report. The women died when a nurse had ordered massive wrong amounts of their transplant drugs, and they'd overdosed.

"I used to work at that hospital and I heard that one of the women was strongly disliked, a troublemaker," posts a woman on the on-line cancer forum I've begun to frequent. *Them, not me. Them, not me*, I chant to myself, a variation on the mantra—*It was her, not me*—that I invoke whenever I hear about the death of a breast cancer patient. *That person is not me. There are many varieties of breast cancer.* The mantra stops the deeper thought—*Maybe it should have been me, in her place. Maybe it will be.* I know enough to identify survivor guilt when it strikes, not enough to prevent it.

Them, not me. But not them either. In the subway, on the way to an MRI, I read the poem that's next to the learn-English ad. "No matter who lives or who dies, I am still a woman," one line goes, and I realize I can never have a thought like that again, with its presumption of survival. I'd have to amend it: "No matter who lives or dies, I am still a woman—unless the person who dies is me, of course, in which case, who knows what I'll be?"

At the hospital, the MRI takes forty minutes. Afterward I follow the twists in the hallway back to the elevator. A Chinese man with gray flecks in his hair gets on at 5, the children's floor. He punches the button hard, swings his arm down, and keeps his eyes fixed sideways, as if to look up could make him cry. In the lobby, I pass a fat man in what appears to be a yachting ensemble. At other hospitals, people usually look rumpled. In a cancer hospital, they're overdressed, sartorial disavowal that anything bad is happening.

Sloan Kettering is a labyrinth, but by now I know my way around. I know, for instance, that there's a cache of phones in Urgent Care that's always available, presumably because everyone's too sick to get up and use them. I know that the shuttle van to the Breast Center, where I have to go next, takes forever, but the walk is quick, ten minutes. I push through the revolving door. Out on the street, a gorgeous bald woman, vibrant in bright orange lipstick and John Lennon sunglasses, holds a paper over her head to shield it from the sun.

"I'm tired of the chemo," I tell Antonelli after the exam.

"Your blood work tells us you're tired of the chemo," she says. "Your white counts are low: two-point-five. Between four and ten is normal. I won't give you the full strength next time."

Blood counts correlate to mood. When my counts are low, depression rubs against me, like a cat. I'm down now, exhausted— too tired to talk to anyone for long, to read, or cook, or do much of anything but put in a daily appearance at work. Lambrakis has given me a serum, Neupogen, to boost my counts, a subcutaneous injection. At home I pinch my belly and push the needle in. The Neupogen helps, but it can't fix everything that's wrong. My eyebrows have thinned to wisps. The right one is nearly gone. The wig is hot and makes me itch. The drugs are producing what's known as chemo brain. I call Judy to find out what time we're getting together that night, leave a message, forget and call again, learn our plans are for Thursday. Chemo brain. Or: All the takeout menus are missing, the ones I keep tacked to the bulletin board. About to write a sharp note to the cleaning woman about throwing papers away, I remember—I put them in a file somewhere. This is your brain, on chemo.

"Not that great," I say at the next support group meeting when Reverend Jacqui asks how I've been.

"I am so glad to hear you say that," she says. "I worried about you last time, when you said you were fine."

But I was fine, within context, I protest.

She smiles weakly. *Suuure.*

Tonight an unfamiliar woman has joined us. Introductions are made. The stranger explains she has multiple sclerosis but is here because she's more interested in cancer. Reverend Jacqui beams, as if this makes excellent sense. Everyone else nods slowly. The woman watched a mind-body special on TV, she says, and was drawn to the women with cancer. She's tried MS groups, didn't like them. She'd rather be with people with cancer.

A half hour in, I'm not so sure she wasn't ejected from the other disease group. "At least with cancer, there's light at the end of the tunnel," she sighs in an annoying manner as people try to air their worries. "You at least have hope."

That you'll leave the room, I think, sneaking another glance at our group leader. Shouldn't Reverend Jacqui suggest that the woman rejoin her people? But the Reverend Jacqui doesn't seem to mind the cross-species pollination. "That's not how you *have* to handle things!" she's busy counseling the MS woman. "Everyone has their own way!"

Topics we cover that night include: the wrong things people say to people with cancer (and MS); the toll cancer (and MS) takes on relationships; the misguided assumptions made about cancer (and MS). When the bipartisan approach grows too cumbersome, we simply talk: about Frances's new puppy; Susan's newly blossoming love affair, which came along unexpectedly two weeks before and has already proceeded to sex. "We were making out and I said, 'I think I should tell you that these breasts aren't real,'" she reports. "'It doesn't matter to me,' he said." He probably thought she meant a boob job, everyone agrees. Then we lie on the floor, close our eyes, and feel the yes! current, not the no! current.

Outside, cold rain pelts us as Frances and I look for a cab. "Are you coming back?" she asks. I'd already confided my apprehensions about Reverend Jacqui. She'd laughed and told me I wasn't alone. Several group members have voiced doubts.

"I don't think so," I say. "But maybe I could meet everyone afterward for dinner?"

"We could," she says.

We do. Before long I get a call from Reverend Jacqui. She hasn't seen me around. Am I coming back?

"No," I say, allowing a silence to stretch between us.

"No?" she asks.

"Nope," I say, pleased at myself for not stammering out a reversal at the sound of her voice. I've shown her: I'm no pushover. But as soon as we hang up, my shoulders droop. I haven't shown myself. She gave me an opening—why didn't I take it? Why didn't I say anything? Why don't I ever say anything, or when I do, it's too late? Did I stand up to the Freudian, or the horrid lab technician, or the officious oncologist? Hardly. One "No" to a mail-order minister does not reverse this record.

I'm no warrior. I'm the cancer patient who plaintively asks for help with a door. I'm the idiot girl who stands stupidly in the clearing, about to be attacked by a lion. Forgetting the end of the dream—the girl killed the beast with just a laugh—I decide: That's it. I've had enough. From now on, I'm the lion.

When the insurance company refuses to pay for my wig, I growl. "Do you mean to tell me you would force a cancer patient to go around bald?" I write back, after a letter arrives denying my claim on the grounds that I was reimbursed for a prosthetic wig already, four years before. "I did not know I was going to get this illness back, or I would have kept the old wig." Within three weeks, a check for fifteen hundred dollars comes in the mail.

I spark a fight on-line, on the breast cancer forum. Since I've gone on chemo, the forum has been my bedrock. The people who log on are mostly funny and smart. They trade recipes for hot-pepper hard candy, to cauterize mouth sores. They explode in cybercheers over triumphs. When Kara reports she celebrated five years' clean by throwing a party and wearing a pig-ear hat ("to show I'm cured"), the congratulations pour in; I have to scroll for an hour to read them all. They comfort and encourage one another. "What's the matter? Can't sleep?" Angelo, whose twenty-nine-year-old daughter has inflammatory breast cancer, E-mails me at three A.M. when I'm up and reading posts. "Shouldn't you go to bed?" The paternal concern calms me and I do.

They divide up and go at one another's throats when I tell off a woman who's launching a single-minded crusade against bone marrow transplants. If it's true that community only ever forms around affliction now (twelve-step groups, families of plane crash victims that hold reunions), in this invisible but very real town, the woman is the local ranter. Reading her posts is like listening to a street person babble: ". . . one little-known fact is that transplants result in liver cancer in 28 percent of the cases, and proponents don't want you to know, but participants rarely recover . . ." In all my investigations into transplants, I've never come across mention of liver cancer. I have a hunch she's pulling facts out of the air.

"... A woman I know is still in bed a year and a half later, her immune system never came back, I went to see her, she couldn't get out of bed ..."

"Her friend probably pretended she was on her deathbed so she would go home," E-mails Joanne, a woman I correspond with privately. When anyone challenges the transplant obsessive, she turns rabidly argumentative. People sometimes meekly question her assertions. But by and large, everyone except Rick Harrison, an oncologist from Tennessee who gives brilliant pro bono counsel, steps around her. Rick posts withering replies, but she's never deterred.

"What does she do in real life?" I write Joanne.

"You won't believe it," she replies. "Some government agency just hired her to write a pamphlet on bone marrow transplants."

One night, when exhaustion is at my throat, I come upon another cracked argument. Too much. I'm too tired. I should go to bed. I don't. I write back and tell the woman to shut up, just shut up, nobody wants to hear her, but as soon as I press "send," I regret it. Freedom is a prerequisite on the forum, even for the crazy lurking man who likes to warn that our bras are causing cancer. I'm out of line, and the village lets me know. Flaming messages land in my E-mail box. A brawl erupts, a melee over transplants and censorship and the purpose of the Internet, that spills out of the cancer forum and washes up onto the Breast Center at East Sixty-fourth Street.

"Hear you started a little trouble on-line," Antonelli says, grinning, the next time I go to the Breast Center. Another forum habitué has been in for an appointment.

My chagrin lasts maybe a day. Soon I'm ready for restraints again.

"Are you having a baby?" a woman asks in the locker room of the gym.

"No, and didn't anyone ever tell you not to ask something like that?" I glower, pulling my arm across my stomach. "I think you're rude."

"No, no, no. I didn't mean—I meant your magazine," she says, her face turning as red as a person's in a step class.

I look down. A bright-eyed newborn smiles up at me from the cover of the newsweekly I'm holding.

"Oh—I'm so, um, so sorry," I stutter.

I'm trying to be sleek and tough in order to trounce the jerks, and all I'm doing is acting like a jerk. I'm clumsy. I over-shoot. I can't get it right, until I hit up against the social worker in charge of transplant patients. I'm unprepared for her nasty intractability because everyone else at the center has been aston-ishingly kind. "I think they haul them off to a back room and force-indoctrinate them into niceness," I tell a friend. "It's weird. When you go there, it's like you're not in New York or something."

But the transplant social worker definitely slipped in off the mean streets. My first clue of this is that she never returns calls. I try once a week, twice, daily. No response. After a month, I ask Jean to speak to her. The next day, the transplant social worker phones. She does not sound happy.

Can she fill me in on insurance procedures? I ask. I'd been told she's the one to ta—

"No. I can't. I don't know about that. You should call your company."

Well, can she give me some idea of how long I'll be out from work? I need to tell my bo—

"No. Everyone's different."

Then can she suggest things other transplant patients have done that were helpful?

"Umm, no," she says. "Uh-uh. No. I wouldn't know." I'm sure I'm imagining it, but I think I hear the buzzy sound of an emery board on nails.

All right. Then here's something I really need. I've been told she's the one who can hook me up with live-in care. I have to get someone lined up. They won't take me into the transplant program unless I have help, and Lambrakis said—

"Why don't you just ask around?" she says. I envision her holding out her hand, for inspection. *That new Korean place has the worst colors. No decent reds at all.* "Why don't you network?"

Because my acquaintance with medical workers is limited, I say slowly, the flame beginning to flick. Whereas hers is supposedly wide.

"You know, people feel like they can plan for this and it will make it all all right," she says. *Damn that manicurist; square was a huge mistake.* "It won't. It's too immense. Everything will work out somehow. I'm telling you this because you seem to feel like you have to control everything."

To my absolute surprise, I turn muscled and tough, without even trying.

"Uh, I don't think I'm overly controlling," I begin. "If you're getting that impression, it may be because you couldn't be bothered to return any calls, and I had to get your coworker to intervene."

"Look, you cannot—" she says.

"No, you look," I say. "The transplant is weeks away. I need to get a caretaker lined up. You are supposed to find me someone, not lecture me on my attitude."

She can't see it, but my mouth has gone slack. *That was me?* Or maybe she can, because she instantly lapses back into her sludgy morass and I end up having to find my own health aide. I, yes, network. It almost doesn't matter. I've taught myself how to roar and it's an extraordinary sound, a crescendo, really, of joy, in claiming pride of place. Once I know how, I rarely keep silent again. Because there's nothing worse for the immune system than getting fighting mad and not fighting.

"Who cares?" I say several years later to a friend, who's bemoaning her single state.

"But society looks down on women if they're not partnered."

"You have a great life," I reply. "Who cares what society thinks?"

"Easy for you to say," she says, laughing. "You got the transplant exemption. Society lets you off the hook if you've had something like a transplant."

"Is that what I got?" I say, laughing, too. "I thought it was Thiotepa."

What I got, among other things, was the ability to roar, and the knowledge that anyone can. You don't need a transplant, or permission, or, even, to lose your fear. To begin, all you have to do is open your mouth.

ROCK

EVERY DAY FOR FOUR MONTHS I WEAR A HAIRPIECE, THEN one day I don't. You wanted to be the kind of woman who would go out without a wig, I think one Sunday night. Well, here's your chance. The following morning, I'm at my desk bald. In truth, I'm not demonstrating courage or defiance or the fact that cancer patients have nothing to be ashamed of. I'm hot. Spring had exploded like a cheer, and summer has followed with its own Bronx variety. New York is a hermetically sealed cauldron, the sludgy air made leaden by pollution.

By now, July, I'm trudging through mornings in a haze of exhaustion, then going home early and drowning in sleep. I'm fed up with being sick, of being perpetually hounded by inconvenience, like when I go to the gym and have to worry about my hair sliding sideways. Once, in the weight room, where all the pumped-up juice boys were hoisting and grunting, I lay down on a bench with some three-pound weights and my wig promptly fell off, exposing my scrubby head. Mortified, I jammed it back on, but I wasn't sure if it was on straight. Without a mirror, I couldn't tell. "You'd better move it," the guy next to me said. "Okay," I muttered, repositioning the bangs. A silence followed. "Excuse me," he said, "I'm going to lift this"—and he patted weights the size of wagon wheels, hanging on a rack near my ears—"so I think you better move the bench, or it could come down on you."

My hairdo, when I sat up, was cocked to the left, as if it was turning toward the wall in embarrassment.

"I thought that was bad hair, not a wig!" Diego exclaimed the first time he saw it, when he came to pick me up after an MRI.

"Diego, censor yourself," I said.

"No, no, it's good," he said. "I did not think that was a wig, only bad hair."

The wig was doing half the job. "I am so sorry I said that," Michelle had begun one morning call. Now that I'm on chemo, many of my phone conversations start this way: *I'm so sorry I said: That thing last night about NutraSweet being carcinogenic. That Tina's mother is sick. That I got a free shampoo sample in the mail.* People's voices quaver as if they've been up half the night kicking themselves in bed. It's only my nicest friends who say these things, which are always inscrutable to me until we've finely deconstructed our last conversation. *Remember, remember, I said . . .* They sound so distressed, I am very careful never to laugh.

Michelle, in this instance, was so sorry that at a baby shower she'd said my hair looked longer. "Your wig is so natural, I forgot."

Really, not a problem, I tell her. But when we hang up, I consider: This ratty toupee does look like I've grown it myself, and it does look pretty bad. Wouldn't I be better off without it? Not long after, I lose the hair. It's as easy as floating into a deeper realm of the sea.

On the street, almost no one gives me a second look. In my world, almost everyone cheers me on. "Sinead!" they say. Or "You're so brave." Or "You really do look beautiful." I love it. It's a shortcut to bolstering, which I really need. Someone from the support group has died, someone my age, and I'm lost in chemo, unable to go back on my decision to stop the hormones and start nuking, not sure I can go forward anymore. My bald head represents my refusal to let cancer oppress me, I try telling myself, but the warrior stuff won't fly anymore, not even with me. Lambrakis has called to say I've cleared the tests, I'm in, I'm going to have a transplant. I'm horribly and profoundly scared.

That's when Laura calls up and offers to teach me to meditate. Someone I know through the magazine, she's had several bouts of breast cancer and is doing fine, a state she attributes, in part, to meditation. If the opinion comes from her, I respect it. Laura's written a book about the brain, knows her Eastern and Western religions, and when she talks about cancer as a spiritual journey, she's smart enough not to sound like she's burping up a bad New Age book. Meditation bores me silly, but I have a whole lot of time on my hands, so I say, "Sure, great." After explaining the techniques, she gives me the rules: Practice twice a day, phone in once a week.

On Wednesday nights I phone, and we fall into great, roiling conversations, like two anchoresses sprung from our cells. We rush past meditation to get to cancer, theology, and death. As badly as I needed to, until she broached it, I hadn't figured out a way to talk about death with anyone, unspeakable as it is in this culture. You can't exactly turn to your friends over dinner and say, "Excuse me, could we change the subject for a second here and talk about my maybe dying?" In support groups, the mention is dicey. If another woman isn't ready to discuss it, you risk deeply disturbing her by bringing it up. As I approached the transplant, though, death was constantly on my mind. I felt like someone whose boss had said, "There's an eighty percent chance we'll be transferring you to Peru within five years, but keep it to yourself."

Laura has no problem talking about Peru, or anything. Will I know what to do if I have to die? I wonder. Umm, millions of people have done it, she muses, and I have to refrain from wise-cracking. "I've seen some beautiful deaths," she adds, making me jump. It takes a while before I can think of death as anything but an aberration or a failure.

Not all our conversations are Andean. Sometimes we compare notes.

"I feel like I've been ejected from my age group," I tell her after a birthday lunch for Claire. Unlike the birthday girl, the other guests only seemed to care about their high-profile careers. I liked my career fine, but felt out of synch; why couldn't they talk about other things, too?

"It's easy to feel like you're divorced from your culture when you've had cancer," she says. "Especially since the culture itself is in the throes of divorce, from illness and death."

Sometimes we just gripe.

"Don't you hate the way they never let you say stress had anything to do with your cancer?" she says in a discussion about official oncological positions.

"I know," I say. "No one would blink if you said you got a cold from working too hard. But if you ever implied stress played any role in your cancer, a support group leader would trample the group to correct you." We'd both investigated the studies. The majority of these hadn't established a conclusive link, a few did implicate stress, and one found that the majority of breast cancer patients thought it had contributed to making them sick, but pooh-poohed them for their belief. "Scientists do not agree," it had quickly added. But Laura and I had seen how far scientists had gotten with the disease. We were going with our gut.

"Yeah," she says. "It's like it's illegal to make any statement that could be misconstrued as meaning a cancer patient caused her own cancer."

If you don't look at what was wrong with your life, you can't change it, one of us invariably remarks at some point during the talk. If I hadn't changed, the other always answers, I bet you for sure I'd be dead by now.

Sometimes we even discuss meditation. Laura introduces me to the concept of the patterned mind. "In India people travel in carts pulled by bullocks, and the carts go along these deep, well-worn grooves," she says, drawing an analogy with consciousness. "People can nod off, so sometimes rocks are placed in the grooves, to jostle them. Many of us are half asleep. The rocks"—life's upsets, obstacles—"keep us awake." Meditation can help you to deal with the rocks, she tells me.

"I've been thinking about how you were brought to the brink of a transplant, then told you were all right," she says. "I'd say that was a pretty big rock."

One Wednesday when she calls, I'm crying. "Bone marrow transplants aren't the magic solution we thought they were," Lambrakis had cautioned me that afternoon. "They only help a small number of women. They're more helpful when there's less bone involvement." He'd paused.

"You have multiple involvement," he'd said.

"But I'm telling you, I have a good feeling about the transplant," I'd argued. He didn't answer.

"Damn him," I say to Laura, so angry I'm blubbering. "I know I'm going to do well, and he won't say it." As focused as an athlete in training, I've reached the eve of the match and the coach has said, "I'm not really sure you're going to make it tomorrow." But what do I want, a doctor who says, "Oh? You know psychically that you're going to be okay? Well, let's just start that transplant now, then, and order the cake for later"? Intuition is crucial to healing, both for doctor and patient. Is it the doctors' fault if protocols and training have purged them of it, if the threat of litigation forces them to give safe responses? I need a pep talk. Lambrakis can only deliver the stats.

"This is a nightmare," Laura says quietly. "You're living in a nightmare." And just the act of someone confirming what I feel brings relief.

"Don't cling to the illusion that this is real," she says, citing Eastern beliefs. "Of course, all of life is an illusion, but this stage of yours is particularly an illusion. You're being tested and will come out stronger, a healer." Laura often refers to tests of strength when we discuss my illness. "You've had a lot of them," she says, and I feel like a circus freak—"Come see the strong man, the lady tattooed by hardship"—but also, secretly, consoled. *This is just a test.*

"I think you're going to make it," she repeatedly says. "I just have that feeling."

Another Wednesday, I ask her about a book. "Have you ever read *The Battle Against Cancer*? I picked it up last weekend, at Graymoor." On retreat with a friend at a Franciscan monastery, I'd contributed to the brothers' upkeep with extensive transactions at their bookstore. Thomas Merton's *The Seven Storey Mountain* now tops Mordechai Richler's *Best of American Humor* on the side table.

"I stopped reading illness books that have the words *battle* or *war* in the title," she says. "It's such a militaristic way of looking at it. So long as you think of yourself in battle with cancer, you'll never transcend cancer. You'll always be engaged with it."

Some nights, when there's too much else to talk about, we nearly forget the purpose of the call. "I guess I should ask if you meditated this week," she remembers to inquire before we hang up. Always, unless I've been too high on Dilaudid, I have.

In the living room, dark except for the light of one candle, I fire up a stick of jasmine incense, sit cross-legged on the futon, and close my eyes. Repetition is polish for ritual. Through practice, my meditation, and my life, acquires luster, even though, most nights, my mind wanders from the mantra inside of five minutes. It makes a beeline for the office, then creeps into mazes that are so pleasing to explore, I'm reluctant to coax it back. When I do, it bounds out like a puppy, eager to display what it's found. Random thoughts are laid before me: "You have to sift through a lot of mud to find the lotus," I hear the chi gong teacher saying. "Music is sustenance," an inner voice observes.

Once, I'm distracted by the sensation of a sweetness so concentrated, it makes me ache. "I've heard people mention that happening," Laura says. "You know what the sweetness supposedly is? Your essence."

The more we talk, and the more I meditate, the more gentled I become. Happiness comes nosing around again. I don't even need to summon or create it. It finds me. In some Hindu sects, happiness is considered to be the highest form of worship, Laura observes. Gladness courses through me like a prayer.

In this contemplative state, lessons pop out from strange, musty corners. Even chemotherapy becomes a teacher. I'd never thought much about drugs' effect. I'd just assumed they have an immediate impact, then vanish in a day or two. Now I notice how chemo—like divorce, mourning, all things drastic—stays on till it melds with you. For weeks after the injection, you can detect its path as it trails through the body, destroying cells and stamina. Four days later, bone pain. Ten days later, exhaustion. It's been my nature to be reckless, to underestimate the half-lives of all forces, benign and noxious. Taxol forces me to pay attention, to respect the drug's lingering power, to consider what the long-term effects of other substances or experiences might be. "All events are the seeds of future events," it says in one of the Buddhist tracts the corner vegetarian restaurant gives customers to read while they're waiting for their orders. I hope that chemo teaches me to plant wisely.

Through the rest of the summer, my baldness seems like an expression of the internal sanctuary I've come to inhabit, a state of grace that continues through the final Taxol. "Do you have your cap and gown ready?" Joanne E-mails the night before. I do: cap, gown, and wig. I've decided to wear the hairpiece so I can pull it off and toss it into the air at the end.

On the last Taxol Friday, three friends accompany me to the chemo cubicle. They duck out or press up against the walls when my usual nurse, Hindy, comes in to start the drip. The first blast is Benadryl. It makes me floaty. The Taxol, next, turns me red.

"Is that air in the line?" Anna says worriedly. "Do you have any-thing for a sugar buzz?" my friend Joe, who's been passing out chocolates, asks. At noon we make a meal of tofu sandwiches and flaxseed salad, and more chocolates, for dessert. At one o'clock Hindy returns to check the IV.

"Ten more minutes," she announces, dropping the tube.

The plastic bag narrows. Five minutes drag by. Seven, eight. Nine, eleven the bag collapses. My gladness peaks. First my spir-its are airborne, then my wig. I am mutant Mary Tyler Moore.

"That's it!" I shout.

"You're done!" my friends yell. We're whooping it up so loudly that if we weren't about to leave, they'd probably have to ask us to.

"Don't take this the wrong way," Hindy says when I find her to say good-bye. "But I hope I never see you again."

"Me, too," I sniffle. "Thank you so much."

This last hurrah's so ebullient, I forget that it doesn't represent the conclusion, but the start. I've got one month off. Then the transplant begins.

Lambrakis calls. They've chosen the date. When we hang up, I log on to the forum. "I'm scheduled for August twenty-fourth," I announce. "I'll go in on a Thursday for the first of two Cytoxans, stay through Sunday, get to be home for two weeks in between. After Cytoxan, they'll bring on the tough stuff: Thiotepa.

"They do transplants outpatient here. Outpatient! I can't believe it. It sounds like the equivalent of a doctor coming to your house and performing open-heart surgery on your living room table. They make you take cabs back and forth to the hos-pital, and only keep you overnight for chemo and any fevers. It's a way to keep insurance costs down, I'm sure. But my doctor swears the rate of infection isn't any higher than when they put people in isolation. My emotions are high-speed mixed. I'm delighted we're starting, also scared to death."

Applause and assurances pour in. "Great news to know that you're moving ahead!" Joanne writes. "I had two BMTs last year," another woman posts. "Both went well although I had a completely different set of reactions to each. One week after the first I did the Susan Komen 5K race (I'll admit it, I walked). I have had some fatigue and various minor difficulties since but it was worth it for me."

Even the anti-transplant crusader weighs in with encouragement, E-mailing an olive branch: "I find myself sharing the hope that the treatment will go really well, that you'll recover very quickly, and that the result will be a complete and lasting remission. We'll all be pulling for you and if wishes and hopes can help, you should get a lot of that kind of assistance, from me no less than the others."

The month off is more like a parole than a reprieve. I thought I'd had every procedure known to oncologists, short of the transplant. But Lambrakis has a couple more surprises in store. He schedules an operation for a second catheter, a loud, embarrassing variety called a Hickman, nothing like the demure bump that's the Mediport. After my head's cleared from the Versed, I see I've got a white, capped hose dangling down my chest, like a backward Chatty Cathy doll. When I tentatively pull on this string to test if the thing's secure, it hurts and makes me say, Fuck.

He gives me a couple of weeks to rest up, then sends me in again, for extraction of the bone marrow that will be reinjected after high-dose. "The bone marrow harvest" is the jolly official name for this step. In between the two surgeries, I spend four mornings at the hospital having a dialysislike procedure called leukoferesis, in which the boisterous new catheter is used to filter stem cells out of the blood. The stem cells, immune-system concentrates, will also be reinjected later, as further boosters.

Leukoferesis, which takes three hours each visit, is noteworthy for its tedium, nothing more. The only painful aspect is having to listen to dueling television sounds from the small black monitors above the beds. Furniture hucksters squawk about enormous discounts. Remote newscasters cajole bleary-eyed patients and family into *concern* for the state of the world.

Closing my eyes, I try to meditate and overhear a Philippine nurse enthuse about transplants to a research fellow from Spain. "The first one we did, Francesca, eight years ago, she was so sick from cancer when we first saw her," she says. "When she came back six months later, no one could recognize her, she was so healthy." I wait for the punch line. There isn't one. Francesca, she reports, is still alive.

The research fellow stops by my bed. He's shy and curious, polite. Handsome, too. I develop an immediate crush, which deepens to potential love when he says, "There are so many new treatments coming along. Every year, everything changes. The best advice I can give a cancer patient is to just stay alive."

If I make it through the transplant, that's my plan, exactly.

After the second Cytoxan, I forget to sing the river. I'm too distracted and, eventually, too sick. But friends, seen and unseen, circle me, in a chorus. I need to have a fleet of friends, I'd thought sadly when I first found the lump. Now I do.

The week before I entered the hospital, presents arrived in the mail from the forum gang: a book by a 1930s humor writer named Thorne Smith, a good-luck ear cuff in the shape of a lizard. The phone rang continuously with offers of help, promises to visit. At the magazine, the editor arranged a lunch to see me off. The staff gave me CDs and cards and a blue-velvet hatbox filled with makeup. "It's the good stuff," the beauty editor said.

My parents drove up. We went to the hospital together. My parents waited in the large reception room while I was brought to a back office and given forms to fill out. They came upstairs with me and remarked on the view from my room. "Why, isn't that nice," my father said, even though all that was visible was just rooftops. A nurse came with a blue Gemini pump, and I took charge, loudly and responsibly asking questions. I didn't want my parents to know I felt a little ashamed to have them see me reduced to this.

The nurse popped a needle into the right catheter, and after that, my memories become sketchy. They've been erased less by trauma than by the drugs that were given to do just that.

Sometimes now, a slice from those months comes back: The night a keening went up outside my hospital room and I crept through the flicker of TV light to see the family spilling out into the hall. "Oh, she was old," the nurse said the next day when I asked who had died, probably to assuage my fear, but making it sound as if old age lessened the importance of death.

The afternoon I couldn't make it to the bathroom fast enough, and the janitor had to come—shades of second-grade shame. The nausea brought on by high-dose chemo was nasty and sharp, even muffled by high counterdoses of an anti-nausea drug called Nystatin. It made me feel as if I had a pack of rabid dogs under sedation in my stomach.

The way a fever lit into me after the big catheter got infected, causing an emergency and chills so severe, my teeth rattled. "You looked like someone in the last stages of AIDS," Diego says. He was there when the nurses rushed in and wrapped my body in blankets and my head in towels. He wasn't when they raced me down to surgery. "We can't wait to give you the anesthetic," I remember the surgeon saying, although burning with a fever of nearly 103, I may have hallucinated it. "We have to get this thing out." I had no immune system. The germy device could have killed me.

"You were like the walking dead," Diego says.

The zombie memories are mostly lost to my brain. But having brought my laptop with me to the hospital and home again, I do have a kind of epistolary record of those two ghostly months. Rereading cancer forum correspondence from that time, I found that Thiotepa turned my skin brown (*it did?*) and left me weak, but spared me the worst of its side effects—mouth sores so severe, morphine and intravenous feedings must be administered. I discovered that during the first half of the transplant, I employed bravado to quell fear. This was not so bad, I announced to the forum. Just got released from the hospital and went straight to a baby shower, in fact. During the second half, bravado was annealed by the despair of exhaustion. To keep myself going, I would conjure the future—after this was all over, I wanted to cycle through Turkey, I wrote Joanne—and when I couldn't, when the relentless present bore down too hard, pushing me under, friends stepped in and imagined it for me. "I guarantee you will drink in life once you start getting your health back. This lousy feeling is temporary," a transplant survivor from Ohio E-mailed me in late September, just after the second Cytoxan blast. "In fact, I figure you and I need to have a drink together down the line to celebrate. How about Friday, October 27th, 1 pm EST? You pick the weapon—champagne, beer, etc. We'll toast each and our ability to get on with life."

"All right—you're on," I wrote back from my hospital bed. "I'm going with the best of what I have—herbal tea. It's either that or Nystatin." Others on the forum said they'd join in, and we talked about the power of healing we'd invoke, but at the appointed time, I forgot and slept through. It didn't matter much, because even if I'd remembered to stay awake for it, the cybertoast would just have made me cry. Everything did, by then.

I'd kept myself pumped up for so long, the crash was inevitable. If I'd allowed myself a wider vision, I might have guessed it was coming. But my sights had had to stay narrowly focused, during the preparatory chemo and throughout the transplant. If I'd calculated possible outcomes—thought, for a minute, that the procedure wouldn't work, or that I might survive it only to wish, at times in the aftermath, that I could die—I never would have done it. And I had to. Not that I had to have the transplant—by the time I was eligible, no one was claiming it was the great salvation anymore—but I had to believe something would save me, even if the agent was only fervor and hope. Even if my only real belief was in the belief itself.

Belief precluded foresight. I could not consider what I might have known: That high-dose chemo, like low, takes out inner resources along with white cells, and that high dose, like low, is cumulative. That by the second month, the build of drugs would thicken in my bloodstream, and the promise of completion would be all that was pulling me forward. That I'd be keeping myself going largely on reminders that there would be an end.

The end became everything, but then it arrived, and the end was empty and cold, dead space.

After the fourth blast, I was in for a week before they said it was over, I could go home. This time I didn't whoop or shout. I was too weak to say much when a friend came to meet me. In the cab we were silent. In my lobby I told her I needed a chair. My legs were too unsteady to wait by the elevator. Upstairs the apartment looked windswept and barren. The thin October light reminded me of gruel. My super hadn't turned on the heat yet and I was freezing. For days I couldn't get warm. I ran hot baths, but the tiled bathroom magnified sound in a way that intensified loneliness. I didn't know how dependent I'd become on the hospital's dozy noise till I heard the faucet drip, as loud in the stillness as a gunshot. Hours went by, and no one spoke to me. No one said, "I'm sorry, I just need to check your line" or "Did you remember to collect your urine?" Something bad could have happened. No one would have known.

Sometimes I took three baths a day, one after every nap. But in the tub, I couldn't escape my reflection in the mirrored bathroom door. If I wanted heat, I had to stare at the hairless creature with a tube hanging down her chest, whose skin was a leathery brown. Nothing resembled me except the bottom of my feet.

When the water cooled and made me shiver, I drained some and replaced it with hot. I would cycle heat until my fingertips wrinkled, or until the dripping faucet sounds ricocheted too hard in my depression and drove me back to bed.

Depression made me pliant. I had no bones. "You're a pathetic cancer patient!" I'd berate myself when the force of the floor pushed on my legs and made them soft wax. "You cannot get to the kitchen! You cannot do anything! You are useless!" I hadn't thought to save my fallen hair to make a shirt, but my bald head served fine.

For weeks after the transplant ended, I stayed in this bleak, black place. In fact, I got worse. The horror of what I'd gone through hung in the apartment like gas. The things that happened, the things I saw, I tried to tell all my friends, but they'd seen them, they'd been there with me. They knew, and I was starting to.

By Christmastime my bones had formed again, enough that I could go out. But my nerves stayed shot. Sobs broke over me at home; in grocery lines I trembled. The wrong noise could make me shake. The wrong thought could lead me to contemplate the advantages of death. This end was empty and so was that; the main difference, as far as I could see, was economic. Life required an expenditure of energy. Death didn't, and I had no energy to give.

"You have just gone through a procedure that cost a quarter of a million, in order to stay alive. You cannot spend that kind of money and then kill yourself," I chided myself one day. The absurdity of this position made me smile.

Oh, lovely, I thought, smile widening to a grin. I don't even have the option of suicide.

My legs got stronger. My cell counts rose. By January I started back at work, half days at first, then full. By February I was no longer shouting at cabdrivers who came to quick stops. In early March I bought a yellow duvet, thinking to cover myself in sun. A few weeks later, out on the street, I caught sight of a goofy, vernalated grin on some guy's face and realized that spring was just days off. Soon after, I noticed it: my hair. Okay, I looked like a Chia Pet sprouting fiber optics—no pigmentation yet—but it was there. Two months later, I had a natural buzz cut, a new mountain bike, and plans to cycle through Turkey in the fall. I'd put my money down before I made my first ride, which was a good thing, because the inaugural spin wasn't auspicious. I barely made it from my house to Central Park, a distance of a mile and a half, when I was ready to call for an ambulance.

"You did how many miles?" a friend asked.

"Um, like, three," I said.

"And you're going to do how many on that trip?"

"Up to forty a day," I replied.

"Oh, really," she said, but I didn't respond. I'd learned how to use the future to pull myself into the future. I knew that I'd make it to Turkey, and I knew that Turkey wasn't really the point. That summer I took a place out in Sag Harbor, at the very end of Long Island, and rode ten, then twenty, then thirty miles a day. It was the only way I could think to exhaust the fury and the fight. *The things they'd done*—pump—*the things I'd seen*—

Slam.

Epilogue

They found the recurrence three years later, one week after my mother died. "I'm seeing something here, on the adrenals," the doctor running the scan said, and to any cancer patient in her right mind, that would have been cause for panic. But my mind wasn't right, then. It was hazy. My mother had spent the year dying—of lung, liver, heart problems, of everything but Parkinson's. I was numbed by grief too fresh to feel. Cyst, I decided, and in the week before the biopsy, I remained in a state that resembled calm. Cyst. I'd had them before. Cyst, no question, of course—if they scanned anyone every four months, they'd find some weird speck somewhere.

Cyst, but what I didn't consider was the timing. If I'd thought about it, I'd have seen that I'd just gone through the ultimate breakup, a divorce more profound and unyielding than any earthly ending. If my instincts had been firing, I'd have known what was coming. But they weren't. It was the only time that cancer has ever caught me unaware.

When she phoned me at the office, Antonelli sounded composed. The results of the biopsy were in. Just one node. But one node positive. No doubt about it, they were sure. "Listen," she said. "I know we wanted it to be otherwise, but I am not very, very worried. This is not in a life-threatening organ. It's still dependent on hormones—it's more of the same, and as far as prognosis goes, that's excellent." The disease hadn't evolved into a more stubbornly resistant form.

"Of course, recurrences are never good," she said, "but if you're going to have a recurrence, you're having it in the best possible way."

But when she phoned my home machine, immediately after we'd hung up, her voice was sorrowful and slow. "I'm calling you now as your dear, dear friend," the message on the tape began. "I am so sorry that I had to give you this news at a time like this. But, you know, I wanted to tell you something I truly, truly believe. You have triumphed in every battle in the past. I have no doubt whatsoever that you will triumph again."

Despite her rousing vote of confidence, I was afraid she sounded as stunned as I felt.

All afternoon I made arrangements—with a pharmacy, to pick up Cytadren; I was going back on the hormone that had trounced the illness before. With Claire, Anna, all my close friends; no way, this time, would I hole up alone. With my boss, for a two-month leave to concentrate on alternative treatments. "We'll do whatever you need," she said, as quickly as she had the first time I'd sat before her and said, "It's, um, it's back." Before I packed it in for the night, I put in one more call, to Rick Harrison, the brilliant Tennessee oncologist from the cancer forum. I wasn't really looking for a second opinion; my trust in Antonelli was complete. More, I wanted a second reassurance.

"Do you have children?" Harrison asked after I'd filled him in at length on my history, the recent relapse, and my concern that I'd be a fool to be optimistic.

"No," I said. Was he suggesting I make provisions?

"Oh. Well—I was going to say, Don't worry, you'll see your grandchildren. But no kids? Okay. Then, in that case, here's my advice to you: Buy the radial tires."

During the next two months, I drank sharp concoctions of carrot, garlic, and cabbage juice. I started on Tibetan herbs. I had injections of Pamidronate, a drug that caused fevers but could help prevent a second spread to the bones. I meditated. I ran. I imagined healing rays of light softening the stiff, crusty node. I was sure, by the time I went for the second scan, that I was kicking that cancer's ass.

"Stable," Antonelli said after the technicians reported back. "I know you wanted it to shrink, but stable is eighty percent good. The cancer hasn't grown, and that means the Cytadren is working. If it weren't, the tumor would have grown." Besides, she said, two months might be a little early to test a hormone's effect. Why didn't we schedule another scan for, say, two months on, see what we found then?

"Stable," she said two months and two days later. "Stable, but this is not a bad result. In fact, I mean it: It makes me very happy. Stable is not what you were after, but I promise you, stable is good."

I must not have sounded as if I shared her rosy vision, because when I returned home that night, I found a message on the machine.

"I wanted to explain why I said I was happy," Antonelli said. "I wasn't just telling you that. First of all, there is a possibility that what we're seeing here is just a scar. It may be the cancer is gone, and if you continue stable, we can find a way to test and see if that's true. But even if the disease is still there, stable is very good."

For one thing, she reminded me, so many new treatments are available or in development, oncologists now consider metastatic breast cancer a chronic illness. Like diabetes, is how they often put it. "People have flare-ups and then they get better," she said. "They continue to lead lives."

For another, she said, my disease had responded to everything they'd thrown at it so far. It was weak and slow and it had gone away in the past, with treatment. With treatment, it would almost certainly go away again. "I know you wanted it to disappear," she said. "But maybe this is better. Cancer that goes away fast comes back fast."

With a slow kind, especially, they could treat it for a very long time, and that's what some oncologists meant when they declared *metastatic breast cancer a curable disease. Not that they could get rid of it for good. Yet. But they could often rout it for extended periods, and when it came back, rout it again. Or they could keep it in stasis, impotent and checked. Antonelli had many patients who'd been walking around stable for years and years.*

"The fact that you keep coming back stable is a really encouraging sign," she said.

"Really," she said. "It's all good news."

Acknowledgments

I complained so much during the writing of this book, I'm amazed I have any friends left, but I do, and I'm extremely grateful to them for their generosity of spirit.

For exceptional good cheer, counsel, and support, I'm indebted to Judy Bachrach, Carol Barden, Martha Barnette, David Berreby, Elizabeth Bradham, Betsy Carter, Joyce Caruso, Susan Cheever, Debra Dickerson, Dana Dickey, Lesley Dormen, Betsy Fagan, Ron Gallen, Elizabeth Graves, Nicole Gregory, Betsy Groban, Joanne Goldberg, Mary Heilmann, Judy Hooper, Jeanne Marie Laskas, Patty Marx, Pearson Marx, Karen Moline, Mary Murray, Christina Oxenberg, Joe Queenan, Michele Romero, Leslie Savan, Michelle Stacey, Judy Stone, Mim Udovitch, Rachel Urquhart, and Lindsy Van Gelder.

On the medical front, I can't say enough for Francis Clifton, Ph.D., and the Faran Center, Violante Currie, M.D., Rick Hankenson, M.D., Sheenah Hankin, Atif Hussein, M.D., the late Angelica Miotti, M.D., George Raptis, M.D., and Antonella Surbone, M.D. Each taught me worlds about the true nature of healing.

Elizabeth Kaplan is a terrific agent and coconspirator. It was her suggestions that got me started and her encouragement that saw me through.

Lucia Quartararo at Crown is a whiz—smart and dogged, a dream to work with.

And above all, I'm thankful to Ann Patty for her faith, vision, and shrewd insights, and for making me laugh at all the right times. That woman kicks ass on so many levels.